Trout & Salmon
FLIES of
WALES

Also published by Merlin Unwin Books
58 Broad Street, Ludlow,
Shropshire SY8 1DA, U.K.
Direct mail orders: 01584 877456

TROUT & SALMON FLIES OF IRELAND
Peter O'Reilly £20 Hb

TROUT & SALMON RIVERS OF IRELAND
an angler's guide, 3rd edition
Peter O'Reilly £16.95 Hb

INTERNATIONAL GUIDE TO FLYTYING MATERIALS
Barry Ord Clarke & Robert Spaight £20 Hb

THE DRY FLY
Progress since Halford
Conrad Voss Bark £20 Hb

CONFESSIONS OF A SHOOTING, FISHING MAN
Lawrence Catlow £17.99 Hb

THE PURSUIT OF WILD TROUT
Mike Weaver £16.95 Hb

A HISTORY OF FLYFISHING
Conrad Voss Bark £25 Hb/£12.95 Pb

OLIVER EDWARDS' FLYTYERS MASTERCLASS
a step-by-step guide to tying 20 essential fly patterns
Oliver Edwards £19.99 Hb (or spiral-bound, direct mail only)

AN ANGLER FOR ALL SEASONS
the best of H.T.Sheringham £16.95 Hb

THE ONE THAT GOT AWAY
tales of days when fish triumphed over anglers
Jeremy Paxman, George Melly, David Steel, et al £16.95 Hb

THE HABIT OF RIVERS
reflections on trout streams and flyfishing
Ted Leeson £16.95 Hb

A PASSION FOR ANGLING
the companion to the TV series
Chris Yates, Bob James, Hugh Miles £16.99 Hb

A FAR FROM COMPLEAT ANGLER
Tom Fort £16.99 Hb

CHALKSTREAM CHRONICLE
living out the flyfisher's fantasy
Neil Patterson £17.99 Hb

Trout & Salmon
FLIES of
WALES

Moc Morgan

Flies tied by
Terry Thomas, Kevin Hughes & Shane Jones
and photographed by Terry Griffiths

Merlin Unwin Books

First published in Great Britain by Merlin Unwin Books, 1996
ISBN 1873674252

Text copyright © Moc Morgan
Photographs © Terry Griffiths

Published by
Merlin Unwin Books
58 Broad Street, Ludlow
Shropshire SY8 1GQ

Tel: 01584 877456 Fax: 01584 877457

British Library Cataloguing-in-Publication Data:
A catalogue record of this book is available from the British Library.

Designed and typeset in Caslon by Merlin Unwin Books
Printed in Great Britain by Bath Press.

Contents

List of Plates

Plate 1
Alexandra, Blackie, Allrounder
Blue Black & Silver (variant), Brown Bomber, Blue Black & Silver Squirrel
Brown & Yellow Mole, Bomber, Closs Special
Conway Badger, Conway Red, Cooke's Bogey

Plate 2
Dai Ben, Dovey Black & Orange, Doctor's Special
Yellow Bumble, Dovey Bumble, Claret Bumble
Fiery Brown Bumble
Earley's Fancy (No.1), Earley's Fancy (No.2)
White Owl, Polly Perkins

Plate 3
Fiery Brown, Wasp Fly, Grey Goose
Harry Tom, Kingsmill, Huw Nain
Lewi's Killer, Mallard & Silver
Marchog Coch, Marchog Glas

Plate 4
Old Favourite, Night Heron, Pry Copyn, Mouse,
Rancid Racoon, Red Mackerel, Silver Grey
Tom Tom, Teifi Terror, Torby Coch
Harries' Sedge, Water Rat & Red
Towy Topper, Twm Twll, Wil Harry's Green Woodcock

Plate 5
Worm Fly, Yellow Plasterer
Treble Chance, Moc's Beauty
Evening Serenade, Midnight Magic, Pussy Galore,
Moc's Bumble, Princess Di, Fiery Jack, Moc's Cert

Plate 6
Black Doctor, Blue Doctor
Silver Doctor, Conway Blue,
Dwyryd Red & Yellow, Haslam, Irt Fly

ix

x

Acknowledgements

━━━━━━

I first looked into the fascinating subject of the history of Welsh fishing flies in 1984. Many people helped me at that time with my research and my debt to them for the present book still stands. Without their outstanding willingness to share their expertise, their insight and their local information (a generosity which I have always encountered in the world of fishing) this book would never have seen the light of day.

The emphasis of this practical reference book, is on the contemporary fishing scene and on the flies that are currently being used on the rivers and lakes of Wales. To this end I have been greatly helped by three superb flytyers, Terry Thomas, Kevin Hughes and Shane Jones. Their combined skills at the flytying bench are visible for all to see in the colour plates of this book. They have an expertise that goes far beyond the production of the flies in this book, for they are also knowledgeable about the way in which the flies have evolved and the kind of angling conditions for which they are intended. I am most grateful to all three of them for their help, at short notice, in getting these wonderful flies tied.

Terry Griffiths took on the task of assembling the flies into plate compositions and has produced a series of photos which admirably convey the qualities of the flies.

I would like to thank Lynn Hughes of Llandeilo for his masterly essay which is published in this book on the origins of flyfishing in Wales and for his commitment, enthusiasm and help with the publication of the precursor to this book, *Fly Patterns for the Rivers and Lakes of Wales*. I am grateful to John Lewis of the Gomer Press for his encouragement and support for the present book.

The following people have, at different times, been helpful to me in providing information about flies, their origins and places of use: Tony Bevan, Llanilar; Ken Bowring, Cardiff; Emrys Evans, Blaenau Ffestiniog; Major T. Ernest Hughes, Llandeilo; Dewi Edwards, Liverpool; Roy Jones, Blaenau Ffestiniog; Dr Graeme Harris, Brecon; W.J. Willians, Llanffestiniog; Emyr Lewis, Llanbrynmair; Norman Closs Parry, Treffynnon; Leslie Peters, Brecon; Tomos Jones, Tregaron; Dave Cole, Tredegar; Hywel Evans, Llanfarian; Father Gargan, County Mayo; Mike Howells, Llanidloes; Dilwyn Richards, Llandeilo; Taff Price, Surrey; Illtyd Griffiths, Capel Bangor; Winston Oliver, Llanegwad; Jean Williams, Usk; Gwilym Hughes, Wrexham; Eirwyn Roberts, Dolwyddelan; John Braithwaite, Bristol; Steve Pope, Bristol; Arthur Owen, Ganllwyd; General Sir Thomas Pearson, Hoarwithy; Harry Lewis, Glyn-neath.

Finally, David Burnett kindly read my manuscript and gave me the benefit of his expert knowledge of flytying as it has been practiced in centuries past and recorded in angling literature.

Moc Morgan, August 1996

Author's Preface

The traditional flies of Wales are not famous for their gaudiness and flamboyance. Indeed (with the exception of the built-wing salmon flies of the last century) there is, in Wales, a strong tradition of tying flies which are dark, dowdy, scruffy, even rough-looking. This is perhaps not entirely surprising for they often have origins in small mining villages, in the remote corners of Snowdonia or the tight-knit valley communities of south Wales, where materials were not bought from expensive mail-order catalogues (as they are now), but snipped from the pet dog under the table or picked off the nearest barbed wire fence. In other words, anglers made their flies from what was locally available and affordable - and what they produced inevitably had a distinctly 'home-made' look. Nevertheless the flies caught fish and that, after all, was their primary function.

In recent years flytyers have been intrduced to a plethora of new materials, many of them synthetic creations which have opened up the opportunities for flytyers no end. Despite this, there is still a discernable ethos in Welsh flytying: that simple, thinly-dressed flies work best - and this tradition is apparent in the illustrations in this book.

This reference book will inevitably reflect my own experience, views and tastes to a certain extent, although I hope that I have included all the important and interesting Welsh flies, and I'm sure my fellow anglers will let me have their suggestions for a future edition! I hope so: it is the exchange of ideas and information which makes the whole topic of flies and flytying so alive and fascinating.

My intention in *Trout & Salmon Flies of Wales* is to look at the flies that contemporary anglers are using and to provide the reader with dressings for them and - most importantly - a clear illustration, so that they know what these Welsh flies actually look like. Every flytyer has his or her own distinctive style and hallmark. The flies illustrated in this book are not the final word but they will, hopefully, serve as an inspiration, and I hope that the reader will soon be at the bench, tying his or her own version of the modern Fiery Jack or the traditional Coch-y-bon-ddu.

Pontrhydfendigaid, Dyfed
August 1996

A Brief History
of Flyfishing in Wales

by Lynn Hughes

Flydressing, that rare combination of intensely practical and instinctive artistry, has a thoroughly absorbing historical development in Wales. It is a genuine - surviving and thriving - vernacular folk art-form which, on examination, reveals local techniques and customs that draw from a general fund of knowledge and contribute back to the flytying community innovations, based on experience, that add scientific and imaginative dimensions.

The Coch-a-bon-ddu and its many variants are known and used by trout flyfishermen throughout the world - from Canada and the USA, to Kenya and New Zealand. It has its origin in the Drop Fly described by George Scotcher for use on the Usk over a hundred and fifty years ago and, by the way its name is tortuously mis-spelled, it is clear that many attribute its nativity either to Scotland or Ireland. Lures now commonly in use in reservoir and lake fishing were, in many instances, pioneered by enterprising Welshmen in an attempt to outwit that wily and still abundant fish, the sewin. Descendants of these pioneers, the present generation of Welsh anglers, have not been slow to adapt the weird and wonderful artefacts of the stillwater fly-box to the purpose of night fishing for sewin.

George Scotcher's delightful classic, *The Fly Fisher's Legacy*, published in Chepstow around 1820, was probably the first book to tackle a subject which he might have called a *'Fisherman's Grand Desideratum, or Long wished-for Instructions'* on flies and fly-dressings, as practised in Wales.

It should, in this connection, be noted that the section on trout-fly tyings in George Agar Hansard's later *Trout and Salmon Fishing in Wales*, (London 1834), is a word-for-word plagiarism of Scotcher's book and is the studiously pilfered piece of patchwork that Scotcher warns his readers against in a declamatory prefatory note headed: 'Caution!'

It is true that some successful anglers are very secretive about their 'killing' patterns - keeping hidden the fly with which they are catching, while talking to a fellow fisher on the bank - but they are the exceptions.

Anglers all over Wales and elsewhere have helped in forthcoming and generous ways to make this book a reality.

But, whatever boastful claims may have been made for certain patterns, where the originals themselves exist, they speak for themselves. The work of Pryce Tannatt, Dai Lewis, Rev. Powell and many others is available for us to see, and the practical worth of their ingenuity is demonstrable. Study of these men's individual contributions, each with their local characteristics, reveals to us aspects of angling custom that are of fascinating interest to angler and naturalist alike. They provide valuable data towards the continuing discussion on the practice of angling in Wales.

In former times, as indeed today, fish and fishing have occupied a special place in the economy of Wales and in the imagination of the Welsh people. When man first settled in Britain some twenty thousand years ago it is in the west and south of Wales that he left earliest evidence of himself, his habitation and way of life. From the artefacts that he fashioned from stone and bone there can be little doubt that the migratory fish which filled the rivers - and the native fish that otherwise occupied the rivers and lakes - provided a seasonal harvest and permanent food source. They were a persuasive factor in determining the positioning and growth of settlements. Shakespeare's Fluellen, in *Henry V*, makes the point when he says that there is a river at Macedon and the river Wye at Monmouth 'and there are salmons in both.'

Shakespeare, well-versed in natural history, might well have known that the first reference to salmon angling was by the Roman poet Martial, who flourished after 43AD: and that Aelian in his *Natural History* c. 200AD says 'I have heard of a Macedonian way of catching fish, and it is this: between Beroea and Thesalonica runs a river called the Astraeus, and in it there are fish with speckled skins. These fish feed on a fly peculiar to the country which hovers on the river. When a fish observes a fly on the surface it swims quietly up and gulps the fly down.'

The metal-crafting people who began to settle in Britain as many years before Christ as we now live after His birth, left coracles, pronged spears and barbed hooks enough in their burial mounds to convince us that they were not only fishermen but had expectation of some fishing heaven which lingers in the race memory of all true fishers! As to what baited these hooks - if anything at all - we cannot tell, nor can we determine precisely when feathers and fur first adorned a hook to deceive a fish - in Wales or anywhere else.

But in Wales we have a fly/fish reference from our literature in the Middle Ages which so pre-dates others as to make it worth a mention here. The greatest of Welsh poets - without fear of contradiction - was Dafydd ap Gwilym, a lusty Cardiganshire squire who was also probably a divine. He flourished between 1320 and 1380 and his artistic genius is matched by his precise observation of nature. In a poem attributed to him, called 'The Salmon', he despatches the salmon as his love-messenger to the bed where his mistress lies with her husband. He refers to the fish as 'gylionwr', 'catcher of flies'

Gwylia yno, gylionwr,

Galw o'r gwely'r gwr.

From it we can deduce that this fly-taking propensity in the salmon was common knowledge in Wales in the fourteenth century and would undoubtedly have been put to use by anglers.

Not until Dame Juliana Berner's *A Treatyse of Fysshynge wyth an Angle*, in 1496, a hundred years later, do we for certain know that fly-dressing and flyfishing were established arts in the British Isles and that the approach to angling entomology was reasonably scientific.

'Fishermen get the better of the fish by their fisherman's craft. They fasten red wool round a hook, and fix on the wool two feathers which grow under a cock's wattles, and which in colour are like wax. Their rod is six feet long, and their line is the same length. They throw their snare, and the fish - attracted and maddened by the colour - come straight at it'.

It was the monks in the great network of priories throughout the country who disseminated knowledge by word-of-mouth and by copying and circulating manuscripts. Tintern, Valle Crucis, Strata Florida and others would know as soon as any one about a treatise on angling from the quill of a distinguished Abbess. The monks all had a vested interest in fish!

Printed books on matters relating to Wales and aspects of Welsh life, other than the spiritual, are scare in the sixteenth and seventeenth centuries. One searches in vain for evidence of angling activity through such sources as the material collected by that greatest of Welsh scholars, the scientist and antiquary Edward Lhuyd, keeper of the Ashmolean Museum, Oxford. Lhuyd, in the mid-seventeenth century, circulated a questionnaire to every squire, parson and literate person he knew in the Principality, requesting detailed information for his projected *Natural History of Wales*. It was, alas, never realised, as he died at the age of 38. Replies that he did receive were published under the title *Parochialia* where there are references to fish but none to fishing.

Delightfully, almost as a marginalium to his great devotional poetry, Lhuyd's Oxford contemporary, Henry Vaughan 'the Silurist', wrote from his home at Newton-on-Usk near Crickhowell, a Latin sonnet addressed to his friend Thomas Powell D.D., of Cantref. It was written to accompany the gift of a salmon and it offers us a brilliant description of an Usk salmon fly c. 1655.

> To the best of men, and his most particular friend,
> Mr Thomas Powell of Cantref, Doctor of Divinity.
> Accept this salmon caught in the rushing weir,
> When he had battled up from the bottom to the topmost waters.
> The false attraction of a simulated insect deceived him:
> A fly made of feathers, painted with colourful markings.
> As he seizes it, he is seized; heedless he swallows,
> And is himself doomed to be swallowed,
> And the catcher of the fatal morsel
> Is made a welcome catch in his turn.
> Blessed rest! the richest reward of this miserable life!
> How safely he could have lain hidden in those still pools!
> As he seeks the roar and tumult of the foaming torrent
> He is swiftly made a prey to my hooked bait.
> What a pregnant emblem of great matters these trifles form!
> The weir is the world; the salmon, man; and the feather, deceit.

Elsewhere Vaughan gives us a glimpse of the idyllic life of the 17th century flyfishing physician in a humourous vignette from a poem composed in 1651 that vies for high honours in terms of the obscurity of its title:

> Thus feasted, to the flowrie Groves,
> Or pleasant rivers he removes
> Where neare some fair oke hung with Mast
> He shuns the South's infectious blast,
> On shadie banks sometimes he lyes
> Where with his line and feather'd flye
> He sports and takes the Scaly frie.

('The Praise of a Religious Life' by Mathias Casuirus. In answer to that ode of Horace Beautus, **Ille qui Procul Negotiis.)**

This is, incidentally, a reference to the sport of samlet (salmon peel) fishing, enjoyed until the present century in ignorance of the consequences in terms of conservation: though in those far-off happy days fish were so abundant in our rivers, that it scarcely mattered.

It is not until the era of the great travellers of the eighteenth and nineteenth century, men who passed through Wales, staying at inadequate inns and lodgings, commissioning engravings and recording their observations in printed books, that we have a graphic record of fish and fishing. The picture is one of rivers teeming with fish and of wholesale slaughter by any method available. Angling was restricted mainly to the leisured classes - people like Rice Mansel, Sir Watkyn Williams Wynn - and early industrial barons such as Crawshay and Guest who owned stretches of the Usk and Wye for their leisure.

Sportsmen in the early nineteenth century complained of being 'glutted with sport'. Thomas Medwin returned from a day on the Teify with his 'shoulders aching with the weight of six dozen trout'. In a previous record in his book, *The Angler in Wales or Days and Nights of Sportsmen*, 1834, he and three fellow-anglers took 500 trout in five days from Tal-y-llyn. George Agar Hansard, author of *Trout and Salmon Fishing in Wales*, also published in 1834, apparently commonly took thirty or forty pounds of trout in a day's angling on Tal-y-llyn and he observes that three or four pound trout were commonly caught above Lampeter where thirty or forty pounds of trout could be taken on the fly in a single day's fishing.

Apart from the depredations of these 'foreigners', a few professional men and a handful of dedicated locals, the fish had it all to themselves. There existed in Wales a certain ethic which identified the huntin', shootin', fishin' element with idleness: call it 'the Nonconformist work ethic'. Fish were there for the taking as food - or as a way of getting your own back on the squire or his keeper - but to spend idle hours angling for them was somewhat to be despised! This attitude undoubtedly has held out in some cefn gwlad 'back of the country' places until well into the twentieth century. A casual survey before 1950 would have revealed a higher proportion of 'church' men as opposed to 'chapel' on the river-bank (in season and in daylight). And it must be said that the romanticisation of the local poacher which survives is, in angling terms, the greatest anomaly in Wales and a real menace in fishery management.

This social aspect, and its divisioning, is curiously important in this study of the fly patterns in use in Wales. The two important elements, as far as the scientific and creative advancement in styles of dressing is concerned, are the keepers and the dedicated locals. The monied classes in the past, as even today, tended to buy their flies and tackle from English and Scottish city stockists who catered principally for the gentry who fished the great rivers of Scotland and the chalkstreams of the south Downs.

Locals in Wales could not afford luxury tackle and very few would have known how to order from Farlow's or Hardy's. To an extent they admired expensive tackle - but also held it in contempt. They themselves held secrets that the gentry and their keepers would not know about, but they would not fail to take note of innovations arriving from London, Redditch, Alnwick or Aberdeen, using ready-to-hand materials to copy them and experimenting, adapting Scottish, Irish and Southern English patterns for their own purposes. In this fusion of knowledge, obviously, the keepers and ghillies played a key role.

Many of these keepers were imported from Scotland and Yorkshire by the aristocracy and landowning classes in order to impose an alien, disciplined policing on a rural society that was steeped in tribal loyalties and prejudices in favour of a common right to the fruits of nature. Such men as Alexander Miller on the Wye or William Law on the Usk and the Barnes family on the Towy maintained an aloofness from the locals which, though always courteous and businesslike, was akin to that social demarcation which exists between Sergeants and senior Warrant Officers and private soldiers and civilians in army life. Indeed, many of these keepers were ex-military men with just such a background.

Rapidly, things have changed. The large estates have, since the Second World War especially, broken up and waters have been sold to syndicates, pension funds and clubs. The old social divisioning has largely disappeared to be replaced by another evil - money. The highest bidder is most unlikely, in Wales, to be a local person - though clubs such as Llanysul Anglers have out-bid all-comers - but club membership itself tends to be far-ranging. The danger is that local knowledge will disperse and be lost: it is therefore important that some record is made.

Local knowledge is what counts in fly-fishing. A pattern that proves deadly one year will not raise even a laugh the following. A fly that kills consistently on the lower reaches is like a racquet without strings higher up. And a fly that catches for one person will not necessarily catch for another. Such is the fascination of flyfishing.

To lose track of some of the traditional local patterns is a loss to angling and to the cultural life of a nation. Hundreds of patterns are, undoubtedly, lost - since flies are perishable objects - and so many anglers were, and still are, jealously secretive of their individual successful patterns. It is to be hoped that, as a result of modern reference books, more will come to light as the importance of recording every aspect of the art and science of flydressing is appreciated.

The patterns that follow are ones that have been tied and tried recently. There is nearly always room for improvement - as a living part of the art. There will always be variations on variations.

It is to be hoped that this publication will be seen as a move in the right direction to encourage others to record some more unknown patterns, by coming forward or by opening up the secrets of their fathers' or grandfathers' fly-cases - before any more is lost to this largely unrecognised art-form.

There is far greater enjoyment in anticipation to be gained from fishing with a pattern that is known to be a fly that has proven itself on a particular water, than to use one bought from a catalogue or a distant shop, which by chance takes a fish. The more so if the fly is the product of one's own workmanship on the bench or tied in the old Welsh method - in the hand.

The Wet Flies

W ere we to rely on printed book sources, there is no really reliable evidence of fly-fishing activity in Wales before 1820, at which time it is seen to have become developed, on the authority of George Scotcher's *The Fly Fisher's Legacy*, published in Chepstow, into being a highly exacting pursuit. There are a number of references to angling in general sporting publications such as Lascelles' *Letters on Sporting*, which, as it were, venture into Wales, but they do not deal specifically with the subject 'from the inside'. Early engravings and poetical citings, dating from the beginning of the 18th century and depicting angling, are not really specific about the method. Typical of these, and exceptionally graphic, is this passage from John Dyer's *A Country Walk* written around 1715:

'And there behold a bloomy mead,
A silver stream, a willow shade,
Beneath the shade a fisher stand,
Who, with the angle in his hand,
Swings the nibbling fry to land.'

It is tempting to think that the 16-year-old John Dyer (who later became famous for another poem, 'Grongar Hill', which describes a feature near his home in Carmarthenshire on the river Towy) is depicting the sport of 'samlet fishing' which, according to Scotcher, was the pursuit of a species caught on two flies with a well-scoured maggot on each hook.

'When they are once hooked get them speedily out, as they are a

1

nimble fish... and you may take from ten to twenty dozen in a day.'

This was before anyone realised that these little finger-marked fish were not a separate species from the salmon and sewin they were destined to become.

But there is every reason to assume that fly-fishing was practised in Wales from the Middle Ages - and when Dame Juliana Berners' *A Treatyse of Fysshynge wyth an Angle* came out in 1496 - her dressing for a Dun fly, in all probability a March Brown, was as well known in fishing circles in Wales as elsewhere in the British Isles. All fly-patterns in use from this period until the early 1880s were bushy flies designed to float on the surface. They were not what we now regard as dry flies.

The distinction between wet and floating fly fishing in times past was obscure, even to those who practised it. Robert Brookes writing in 1740 suggested sinking the fly as much as six inches and Lascelles in 1811, in a letter from Wales, gives a 'tip' for bright days - 'sink the fly a little'. When Charles Cotton, in an addendum to the 1676 edition of Isaac Walton's *The Compleat Angler*, refers to the technique of keeping the fly afloat in a stiff breeze, he seems to be alluding to a generally understood and the most widely-practised tenet of fly fishing - the up-stream floating fly, and not one exclusively pursued in the South of England. It can be surmised that all patterns were tied to float until they submerged and that, like the naturals they represented, they swam until they sank. George Agar Hansard in *Trout and Salmon Fishing in Wales*, 1834, says 'When you flourish your fly on the surface, be sure you gain the head of the stream.' So the up-stream floating fly, it would seem, was still being advocated for trout fishing in Wales at a time when wet fly patterns and techniques were in use elsewhere.

The number of rivers in Wales where the dry fly fishing approach is more efficacious than the wet, is anyway limited - as the geography of Wales dictates fast-flowing, rough waters. Thus, for the most part, Wales is, and has been since the early nineteenth century, a straightforward, up or downstream wet fly fishing place. Stiff, hickory rods did not allow for very subtle casting or presentation until the arrival of greenheart and, later, split-cane around 1860.

Wet flies, or flies that could be fished wet, were fully evolved by the beginning of the nineteenth century. Influences arrived from England. Samuel Taylor in his *Angling in all its branches reduced to a complete science: being the result of more than forty years real practice and strict observation throughout the Kingdoms of Great Britain and Ireland*, (1800), is typical of the day in assuming that the salmon and trout patterns known to him in his wide experience were equally applicable to England and Wales. The northern English flies, as earlier described by Cotton, were eminently suited to Welsh conditions. They were sparsely dressed in terms of hackle, with wings set at a very high angle. They were quick to sink and when retrieved showed a lot of life through the water. Early wet flies are imitations of stone flies, the sedges and terrestrials such as the oak fly and the cockchaffer beetle. They were designed to imitate drowning and drowned insects and those that descend into the water to lay their eggs on plant life and in the mud or gravel on the bottom.

Usk anglers used flies with very slender bodies and very little hackle. Their divided wings were set low over the hook with concave sides set together. These early Usk flies had dun wings and hackles, they had no tails and the body was of wool or hare's ear fur. Scotcher's dressing for the Green Drake however is a little more sophisticated and a fascinating example of early flytying practice. The 'Grey Drake, Tilt-up, or Up-and-Down Fly' was tied as follows:

> 'The wings are made of mallard's feather, which may be chosen exactly to the colour of them; the head either of peacock's herl or ruddy-black sheep's wool, the body of white shalloon, with a very small quantity of pale yellow with it, darkened with ruddy-black sheep's wool at the extremity of the tail; the three whisks as the green drake, and an almost black hackle for legs.'

He, presumably, intended here an artificial to match the oak fly, which is sometimes called the 'downlooker'.

Interestingly, Scotcher remarks at the conclusion of this article on the Grey Drake:

> 'The Green and Grey Drakes are by no means general flies, for several English rivers and most of the Welsh rivers are without them.'

Thus, he makes it clear that there were, around 1800 and earlier, generally known and adopted local patterns, and there were other places where these were either unknown or unfruitful.

In general outline, throughout their history, Welsh wet flies have been streamlined to ensure good entry into the water. As the great Dai Lewis demonstrated, they should swim on an even keel and possess sufficient 'kick' to suggest life. This liveliness is achieved by the all-important setting of the wings and the hackle, so that they spring back against the current when released from the tension of forward movement. This facility for reaction to movement in the current is of vital importance in fast-flowing rivers such as those that characterise the Principality.

Ace of Spades

PLATE 20

Hook: Long shank 8 & 10
Tying silk: Black
Rib: Oval silver wire
Body: Black chenille
Wing: Black hen, tied matuka style
Over Wing: Bronze mallard
Hackle: Guinea fowl

The Ace of Spades works best in cold and rough conditions, and especially at Llandegfedd, Brenig, Eglwys Nynydd and Dinas.

The Ace of Spades is one of the most popular early season lures on Welsh reservoirs. In the early days of the season reservoir trout tend to lurk down very low in the water, so the angler has the problem of getting his offerings down to them at the same level. While it is always advisable to vary the speed of retrieve of a lure, in the early season, it is generally best to move the lure slowly.

As the bottom of the reservoir holds the most food during the early months, getting the lure down as low as possible is difficult from a boat. Use a drogue to stop the boat drifting too quickly - and every legitimate method to sink your fly line to the very floor of the lake.

A hen hackle tied in over the back - in the Matuka manner - ensures that the hackle does not wrap itself around the hook, a common problem with other long-winged patterns.

Alder

PLATE 9

Hook: 12
Tying silk: Brown
Body: Rusty coloured wool

Hackle: Dark blue dun

Pluen lwyd ar gorff lliw haearn
(A dark blue dun hackle on rusty body)

The age-old custom of naming Welsh fly patterns by describing the material make-up of a fly has many advantages. The immediate one being that the angler never forgets the dressing of any pattern. This particular pattern appeared in the booklet, *Llawlyfr y Pysgotwr* (The Fisherman's Handbook), written by William Roberts, and published in 1899. It is a representation of the alder larva.

The alder fly (*Sialis lutaria*) is well known to most anglers. It has a dark head, an even darker body and heavily-marked, rich brown, roof-shaped wings, somewhat sedge-like, but lacking the minute hair covering that is found on sedge flies' wings. It flies to and fro in rather a ponderous manner and could be likened to a helicopter as it chops about depositing its eggs on bank-side vegetation from which, in due course, the larvae fall into the river and proceed to burrow into the mud on the river bed. They spend some ten to twelve months in the river growing and shedding their skin in the process. Then each larva crawls back to the bank and, after locating a soft patch, buries itself for the period of pupation. After ten days it flies away - a fully-fledged insect - to find a mate in the bankside vegetation, before the story starts all over again.

The artificial Alder was extensively used in Wales in the early nineteenth century and the dressing used in those days is outlined in *The Fly Fisher's Legacy* by George Scotcher. In it he says:

'Natural: It has four cloak wings like the green tail fly, of a yellowish smoky colour, strongly paned or chequered with black; the wings rise from the ground in a ridge over the back and body, which they entirely hide. The two feelers, legs, head, and body of the

5

fly are of a dull reddish black, except the under part of the tail, which is first of a blood red and then inclining to a Seville orange colour. It abounds mostly in brooks, or rivers whose sides are wooded by orl or alder bushes, on which, during their season, they are always found, they do not hover over the water like other water flies, but being rather a full fly, are seen flying across and from bush to bush, and on rails by the river's side, running very fast, and frequently fallen on the water. You may use [the atrificial] any time of the day after the sun is well up till evening, and a warm blowing day which beats the bushes about is the best.

'Artificial: Make it with a freckled dark cock's hackle round the top of the shank of the hook, and the body either of ruddy black sheep's wool, with waxed Seville orange coloured silk, or else with a coppery tinged peacock's herl, twisted round the silk and worked on together. As a winged fly, I have made it from the brown speckled feather on a wild mallard's back, a very dark hackle for legs, and the body of chocolate and orange wool, well mixed, tied on with reddish silk.'

Alder (C.F. Walker)

PLATE 9

Another representation of the larva that has been used in Wales is a pattern suggested by C. F. Walker:

Hook: Long shank 10
Tying silk: Brown
Tail: Ginger hackle points
Rib: Gold tinsel
Body: Tapered brown ginger seal's fur
Gills: Sandy hen
Thorax & head: Hare's ear
Hackle: Brown partridge

Scotcher's Alder which he calls 'The Orl Fly, Lifting Fly, Orange Tawney, Orange Brown, Camlet Fly, or Bastard Caddis' is an interesting representation of the natural, but today the Orl in use on reservoirs is somewhat different.

Amber Nymph

PLATE 25

Hook: 10 & 11
Tying silk: Brown
Body: Amber seal's fur tied full for back half of body. Front half, thorax, of brown seal's fur
Wing case: Strip of grey feather tied in at tail and finished behind the thorax
Legs: A few fibres of pale honey hen hackle, tied under the head

Dr Bell, the famous fisherman of Blagdon, was responsible for creating this pattern which has subsequently gained much favour on many fisheries in Wales. It bears a close relationship with the Rusty Spider patterns that were used in the Bethesda area at the turn of the century.

On lakes, the Amber Nymph works best from May onwards and is most probably taken for the pupa stage of the brown silverhorn sedge (*Athripsodes cinereus*). The brown silverhorn sedge is quite a common sedge with very long antennae which look like long horns.

Amber Nymph (L. Sweet)

PLATE 25

Hook: 10 & 12
Tying silk: Brown
Tail: Red hen
Body: Amber floss
Rib: Gold thread with black thread ribbed alongside
Thorax: Amber floss

Hackle: Soft red hen

This pattern is attributed to Lionel Sweet, an expert caster who, with his wife Molly, ran the well known tackle shop at Usk for many years.

Ant, Red (Formica rufa)

PLATE 9

Hook: 16
Tying silk: Red
Body: Red tying silk built up to form two thick sections, a thorax and an abdomen with a thin waist between. Varnish the silk body
Hackle: Ginger cock
Wing: Blue dun hackle tips

A fall of ants on the water on a day will always trigger off mad activity among the trout as they rush to feed on them, often ignoring all other forms of food. An angler is very fortunate if he happens to be out with the rod when the ants fall if he has, or can make up by hand, a pattern that is likely to fool the trout: it need not be too exact as, in their excitement, the trout feed with blind avidity. Many believe that trout are partial to formic acid; if so, it is always a temporary addiction, as they will only feed on ants for a short while and then lose interest completely.

Most anglers who have trout-fished for a number of years will have come across a fall of ants. Why these most organised of insects develop wings and, for no apparent reason, fly off from their nests no-one really knows. Some believe that the flight may be a nuptial one and that after the mating ritual the females return to the nest.

Ant, Black

PLATE 9

Hook: 16
Tying silk: Black
Body: Black dyed peacock quill. Butt and thorax of ostrich herl
Hackle: Cock starling
Wing: Pale starling

The colour of the Ant is not all that important: it is the overall impression of the body shape that matters. There are critical light conditions when perhaps more precise dressing and colour is likely to be effective.

George Scotcher writing around 1820 from Chepstow found difficulty in finding an exact feather to match the wing.

'It is needless to describe the form of these, as they are only the ants or pismires with wings, except that I think their tails are more of a bottle shape at this time.

'*Natural* The wings of the red ant are light and yellowish, the body yellowish brown, and the legs light ginger.

The Artificial, is made from the light-yellow part of a thrush's quill feather, the legs by a small ginger hackle, with the fibres taken off one side of it, and the body from a yellowish herl near the eye of a peacock's feather. I have known the hackle and herl answer better without wings.

'*Natural*. The wings may be made as the others, or from the light part of a starling's wing, for I know no feather that will match it exactly, the body of brown peacock's herl, with a brownish or almost black hackle, or, as said of the other, the hackle and herl alone.

'They come on, in a hot season and low water, about the beginning of July, and generally from mid-day till three or four o'clock, but unless well looked after, are not observed; in a wet season they are entirely lost. Towards the end of August, a smaller sort of fish kind come down, but it requires great nicety either to fish with or make them, indeed it may be said of both sorts, that if not seen in great numbers, they are not worth attending to. I believe no angler ever goes purposely out to fish with the ant fly, but if in this season he should be out and observe the fish rising much, without seeing any fly on, he should then look carefully for them on the eddies, froth, or still water, and most likely will find the rise is at these flies, which he must then throw.'

August Brown

PLATE 9

Hook: 12 & 13
Tying silk: Pale orange
Tail: Cock pheasant strands from tail feather
Body: Two or three strands from cock pheasant tail (light shade), ribbed with gold wire. Two or three turns of bronze peacock herl at shoulder to represent the thorax.
Hackle: Pale honey dun cock and grey partridge dyed beige

Despite the excellence of this pattern (by Pryce Tannatt) in representing the August dun, many Welsh anglers just use a smaller version of the March Brown which is similar. The August dun (*Ecdyonur dispar*), as its name suggests, appears on Welsh waters in late summer, long after the March brown has gone. While the male spinners of the August dun are somewhat like red hot needles, the female spinners are almost identical to those of the March brown.

Courtney Williams gives a dressing for the August Brown attributed to Francis Walbran which the creator held to be a very effective fly.

Hook: 12-14
Tying silk: Brown

Body: Light brown floss silk
Rib: Yellow silk
Tail: Two rabbit whiskers
Wing: Cock pheasant wing feather
Hackle: Brown hen

In recent years there has been a tendency among anglers in Wales to concentrate on the dry fly after early May - even on fast flowing streams. Some, however, do well with the wet fly immediately after high water. The August Brown fished on the point does well in such circumstances.

Baby Doll

PLATE 20

Hook: 6, 8 & 10 Long shank
Tying silk: White
Body: White Sirdar wool
Back: White Sirdar wool

The Baby Doll was first used exclusively on reservoirs and is at its best when the fish are feeding on fry. Using a sinking or a floating line, the lure can be left to float or sink, without any retrieve whatsoever, to make it appear like a dead fry. Others prefer to retrieve the fly, making it dart like a small struggling fish.

The former all-white Baby Doll has now appeared in every colour of the rainbow. Probably the most popular of these variations has a green fluorescent back, called the Peppermint Doll. This variation is used a lot on the Ynysyfro Reservoir near Newport.

Badger Matuka

PLATE 20

Hook: 6, 8 or 10 Long shank
Tying silk: Black
Rib: Silver wire

8

Body: White chenille
Thorax: Orange wool or chenille
Wing: Two or three pairs of well-marked badger hen hackle
Hackle: Hot orange cock

The Badger Matuka is a good lure to use from a boat in September or October on a reservoir. Anchor the boat, cast the Badger Matuka well out and allow it to sink: then retrieve it slowly along the bottom of the reservoir. Trout in early autumn are busy feeding on small fish, which congregate in particular locations known to the big predatory trout. Once the angler discovers these fry then a big Badger Matuka cast in amongst them will encourage and entice a big trout to strike out of a sense of rivalry and invaded property.

The Badger Matuka is also a good sewin lure on a cold night when the swein are hugging the river bed. Used on a quick-sinking line, it can move the sewin to take something that is whipped across their field of vision. Sometimes, when the sewin have been upriver for some time, it pays to try a smaller version of the lure.

Black Buzzer

PLATE 25

Hook: 12
Tying silk: Red
Tail: White hackle fibres - tied round the bend of hook
Body: Black wool
Rib: Flat lurex
Overbody: PVC
Thorax: Green peacock herl

In the last two decades many old Welsh fly patterns have temporarily lost their appeal on Welsh reservoirs such as Eglwys Nunydd and Llandegfedd. The Black Buzzer is typical of late twentieth century fly technology, using newly-available materials - in this instance PVC and lurex - to create an effect, that of capturing an air bubble, which older practitioners of the fly-tying art had been hard-pressed to achieve with baser materials.

Black Gnat

PLATE 9

Hook: 14 & 16
Tying silk: Black
Body: Black ostrich herl
Hackle: Black hen
Wing: Starling or snipe

The Black Gnat was at one time widely used on the upper reaches of the Wye and the smaller streams of mid-Wales. In a collection of top lines dressed by Tom Tom of Cwmystwyth many casts had the above dressing of the Black Gnat tied on the tip dropper, while in the same collection there were a number of black flies tied with black ostrich herl and no hackle or wings.

The black gnat, *Bibio johannis*, is quite a common fly - not unlike the ordinary house fly - but it is not really as black as many anglers may suppose. Some tend to use dun hackle - especially on the dry-fly version of the Black Gnat.

In common with a number of other flies, this artificial will take fish when the natural is nowhere near the water. When there are a lot of the naturals about the trout will feed avidly on them to the exclusion of the everything else.

Scotcher, with characteristic sensitivity, gives this description of a master angler's approach with such a dainty offering:

'*Natural*. Like a small house fly but still much smaller, and the tail part of the body runs taper to a point; the wings are very light and the body dark. They begin to appear early or late in May, according to the mildness or warmth of the season, and are seen hovering in great numbers together generally over the tail or side of a stream, or on some particular part of a still water, where you will see the fish rise at them as they fall in couples on the water. At first they appear about two o'clock and as the cool evening draws on you lose them; after that as the weather becomes hot, they are solely an evening fly from about five or six o'clock till the edge of night, and as the wind then generally sinks in the evenings, you will perceive on the still water where they are by the fish rising at them, and by having a long rod, a light line, with the finest bottom , a small and light wired hook, a neat made fly, and keeping well off the water, throwing gently and with great nicety in the ripple near the fish's rising, in the way you perceive he is swimming, you my succeed, and, but in a moderate way only, unless you are very skilful and use the utmost caution; towards the tail and side of streams your sport is more certain. They continue at times almost all the summer, and should only be used in calm hot evenings.

'*Artificial.* I make it on the lightest hook I can procure of No 12, breaking the shank short, with a very light-blue dun hen's hackle, making the body of a small herl of a peacock's tail feather, the fibres of which should be very short and thinly scattered. When the fish are small, and the river free from any foul bottom, I sometimes tie it on to a fine glass-coloured round hair, and of course the other part of my bottom single hair, which falls excessively light and will lie on the water, and the fly is frequently so taken, but without much practice and care you are very apt to snap it off in throwing.'

Black Lure

PLATE 20

Hook: 6, 8 or 10 Long shank
Tying silk: Black
Rib: Silver tinsel
Body: Black chenile
Wing: Four matching black cock hackle feathers.
Throat hackles: Black hackle fibres

This is by far the most important lure that is used on Welsh reservoirs in the opening days of the season. On opening day 1983 at Eglwys Nunydd reservoir, Port Talbot, over eighty per cent of the anglers were using the Black Lure on a quick-sinking line.

Most reservoir fishing in Wales is from the bank, and the Black Lure requires fairly proficient casting in order to put the lure some thirty yards out into the water. It must then be allowed time to sink, and only when it has sunk properly should it be brought back: and not too quickly.

As the season advances, the speed of retrieve can be increased - and the depth at which it is fished then becomes less critical.

As a sewin lure fished deep and towards the hours of dawn, the Black Lure has no equal. The same principles apply as for the reservoir fishing, except that the later into the night the deeper it should be fished and the larger the size ventured.

Black & Peacock Spider

PLATE 9

Hook: 12, 12 & 14
Tying silk: Black
Body: Under layer of black wool, covered by bronze peacock herl
Hackle: Soft black hen

Tom Ivens's excellent book, *Still Water*

Angling, was responsible in part for spreading the word about the Black & Peacock Spider. Since then, most stillwater anglers have the pattern with them as a general standby and, luckily, it is also one of the easiest of all patterns to tie. It was, however, known in North Wales for at least half a century before Tom Iven's book.

Black flies were very much in vogue at the turn of the century, at a time when most Welsh rivers held amazing stocks of fish. The advice in *Llawlyfr y Pysgotwyr* (Angler's Handbook) 1899, was that wet flies on a cast should be some twelve inches apart. If this is correct, it provides another insight into methods practised some eighty years ago. It underlines the fact that much of the fishing done was on comparatively small rivers. These Welsh flies were tied extremely sparsely and were fished up-river because of the problem of keeping out of the trout's view.

The **Pluen ddu ar gorff paen** (Black feather on a body of a feather from a black hat) uses a black ostrich feather. It was typical of how flydressers at the turn of the century used readily available materials. In this instance the feather came from a lady's hat - as did indeed so many other fancy feathers.

Black Pennell

PLATE 10

Hooks: 4-6 for sewin; 8-10 for reservoir trout; 12-14 for river trout
Tying silk: Black
Tail: Golden pheasant tippets
Rib: Silver wire
Body: Black floss
Hackle: Black

It is generally accepted that an angler cannot go far wrong with a black fly pattern on all Welsh waters, be they rivers, lakes or reservoirs. The Black Pennell is a natural progression from the all-black patterns of the early years.

Black Pennell has an excellent reputation on stillwaters and is a fly that works almost everywhere in Wales - as in the rest of the United Kingdom. It can be depended upon to give the angler an even chance on most waters and is a good standby when one is unsure of what to use.

It has no favourite position on the cast, many anglers use it on the bob while others always have it on the point. On some of the bigger Welsh reservoirs like Trawsfynydd and Brenig it does well when used with a quick-sinking line and fished deep. On many natural lakes it serves well as a bob fly.

It was, some two decades ago, a very popular sewin fly - but this is not so today. On the river Conway it was formerly known to take good sewin; some do still tie it - in tandem form - today.

In recent years, certain modifications have been made to the Black Pennell. Some anglers add a lime-green fluorescent tag to the fly and this is said to help the pattern. Others have palmered the hackle - quite a popular variation with reservoir anglers. The palmered hackle tends to create quite a lively object from the trout's view-point as it bobs on the surface - which accounts for its effectiveness as a bob fly.

Its creator, H. Cholmondeley Pennell, had other Pennell patterns of different colours, the best known of them being the Claret Pennell. Claret Pennell has its addicts on a few reservoirs in the Taff Valley. There are Pennells with green, yellow and brown bodies, but they are not used extensively on Welsh waters.

Black Quill

PLATE 10

Hook: 14
Tying silk: Red
Body: Well marked quill
Hackle: Short black cock

This pattern, in common with many others, is often the victim of poor tying. Many of the commercially-tied examples of this pattern are complete abominations. Often it is evident that little effort has been made to secure well-marked quills. It does not seem to be appreciated that some of the drab quills commonly used detract greatly from the pattern. Some tyers mark the quill with a black felt pen to achieve this striped effect. Unless this is done to perfection, the contrast between the black and the white part of the quill will be seen to be lacking. On choosing material for the quills it is always wise to inspect the hind side of the peacock eye feather. If that is not registering a whitish hue, then it should be rejected. The best method of stripping the flue from the peacock quill is still the old fashioned thumb-and-forefinger method, done quickly against the grain of the flue. Flies made with quill bodies have always been popular in Wales, despite the fact that quill is not the most durable of materials. Some flytyers would use a thin silver wire in order to protect the quill from the teeth of the trout. The red silk was intended to show both at the head and the tail.

The Black Quill has long been used both as a wet and dry fly. It has proved a favourite bob fly on a three-fly cast fished downstream. In days of old, wet fly anglers would hang their wet flies from their very long rods directly downstream - moving the bob fly in and onto the surface of the water. This technique, while it often succeeded in moving a fish, is notoriously poor at hooking

them. The Black Quill used as a bob fly or dry fly is thought to be a good representation of the black gnat.

Black & Silver

PLATE 9

Hook: 12
Tying silk: Black
Rib: Silver wire
Body: Flat silver tinsel
Hackle: Black hen

The old market town of Tregaron on the river Teifi holds an important place in the development of trout fly fishing in Wales. The primary reason for this, of course, is that the famous Dai Lewis lived there. Another great fly dresser too, not so well known, who lived only a hundred yards from Tanygraig, where Dai lived, was Charles Harrison, or 'Charlie' as he was known. Charlie was also a very gifted flydresser, if not such an energetic fisher as Dai. His exquisitely dressed flies are known to decorate angling clubs as far afield as New York.

His favourite fly was the Black & Silver which he fished with great delicacy. He would sometimes add a red tail to the pattern which helped - especially in dark water conditions. The pattern was, otherwise, dressed on a small double hook which helped with the hooking - when used as a bob fly. In recent years the pattern has been tied up in tube-fly form for sewin fishing, and larger versions on Esmond Drury, double hook and Waddington irons are effective salmon lures. In tube form the black hen hackle has been replaced by squirrel hair dyed black.

The simplicity of this pattern belies its effectiveness. Anglers using a Black & Silver tube fly of some one, to one-and-a-half inches long, as does John Mercer on the

12

River Towy, find that it produces excellent results with sewin.

Black Spider

PLATE 10

Hook: 11, 12, 13 & 14
Tying silk: Purple
Body: Rear portion, flat silver tinsel; front portion, three or four turns of peacock sword feather
Hackle: A black cock saddle hackle

The Black Spider pattern designed by Pryce Tannatt has proved to be a more than adequate variant on Williams' Favourite. Some anglers, approving of the silver tag especially, have used it to good effect when fishing the pattern during a buzzer rise. Some of these spider patterns often score better than do the more sophisticated dressings of the buzzer pupa.

The spider pattern was designed primarily to fish on the smaller rivers and streams of Wales. Often the dressing would only cover the upper half of the hook as per the style of a low-water salmon fly. The approach was to dance the wet flies on the surface of the quick flowing water with the long hackle being brought alive by the play of the current. This mobility of the long cock hackle gives the fly a semblance of life and a fascinating colour pattern where the body colour is veiled with the sparkling hackle.

Black Spot

PLATE 10

Hook: 14
Tying silk: Black
Body: A small ball of black rabbit fur wound close to base of hackle
Hackle: White cock dyed dark green

This pattern was devised to suggest the gnats and midges on which trout often feed on 'difficult' evenings. Anglers at such times try hard to find a pattern in the box that will attract the trout and the Black Spot often so succeeds. Some fly patterns, although not used often, are an essential reserve ingredient of an angler's equipment to be kept for especially difficult occasions.

Blackie

PLATE 9

Hook: 8, 10 & 12
Tying silk: Black
Tail: Black fibres
Rib: Silver wire
Body: Black seal's fur
Hackle: Black shiny cock
Wing: Black squirrel tail or long hackle fibres
Cheeks: Small jungle cock

This is a very young pattern which has become more widely known and used because of its success in fly fishing competitions. The man who was responsible for bringing it to the notice of the competition circus was Mike Howells of Llanidloes. It is primarily a reservoir pattern for use on Llyn Clywedog, Llyn Brenig and Trawsfynydd. The success of black lures on reservoirs is well known. Blackie, fished on a sinking line, does seem to have the ability to make contact with fish lying on the bottom. Often it is used on a three or four-fly cast and is invariably put on the point. In that position the Blackie is the fly that fishes deepest on the cast and so performs the task of scraping or bumping along the bottom of the water.

Blackie is also a very successful boat fly. Again, used on the point, it takes fish when stripped fast, as is the custom in modern reservoir fishing. Boat fishing on reservoirs that have rainbow trout often produces a situation known as 'bottom pinching' in which the trout follow for a considerable distance, just giving the fly a tweak now and again. Often by moving the fly more quickly the trout can be hurried into being hooked. The Blackie can, more than most, cure this perversion of bottom pinching!

The Blackie in tandem form too, is an excellent sewin fly for use with a quick sinking line.

Bloody Mary

PLATE 10

Hook: 10-12
Tying silk: Magenta
Tag or Tail: Red wool or ibis
Body: Peacock herl with gold at tail
Hackle: Grizzle hackle dyed scarlet

A variation of the Coch-a-bon-ddu, though it is doubtful if it offers an improvement on the original. It has certainly scored recent successes with rainbow trout and, as it continues to do so, it could become a favourite. Most fisheries in Wales now stock with rainbow trout, and so the Bloody Mary could, in time, prove its worth as a bob fly.

It is one of the attractor-type flies that was used on the Elan Valley Lake complex in the forties and was offered to trout that had refused everything else thrown at them - a great test for any fly. It is a totally unusual pattern: and, perhaps, there-in lies the reason for its success!

Recently, the hatches of coch-a-bon-ddu beetle have been more pronounced, and trout in places like Claerwen have been taking them well. After a few days, however, they tend to look for something different: and then it is worth shaking them a Bloody Mary.

Blue Hen

PLATE 10

Hook: 13
Tying silk: Black
Body: Black quill, finely dressed with two turns of black herl as thorax
Hackle: Underwing of moorhen (Summer plumage)

This fly earned the reputation of being an excellent top dropper on a three-fly cast fished downriver. The main drawback was that the trout invariably damaged the quill body. Unfortunately the Blue Hen, like many other fly patterns tied by Dai Lewis, is in danger of being forgotten, and traditional wet-fly fishing is itself being practised less and less as other styles become the fashion.

It is therefore fortunate that some of the more successful river patterns are still being used by stillwater fishers. The Blue Hen has itself been subjected to this transference and is proving its value in its new environment. This change of location has also meant a change of position on the cast. It now operates well on the point position of a long cast. Here, the angler casts his flies out, and allows the Blue Hen time to sink some ten to fifteen inches below the surface before he brings here and the team back by means of the sink-and-draw method.

Dai Lewis tied flies commercially and there was a great demand for his productions outside the Principality. A large number of Blue Hens went to tackle shops in the North of England where they must have worked well for discriminating northern customers.

Blue Ruff

PLATE 10

Hook: 14
Tying silk: Green
Body: Heron fibre or green wool
Hackle: Pale to dark blue dun hen, or pale to dark olive hackle

This is another fly from the river Usk. The pattern was given to the Editor of *The Field* by a Mr Acheson who was a keeper on the Usk. The herl body was used on a number of flies and, with the green silk, made a good body to represent the olives. It was generally used as a dropper and fished when olives were hatching in the early part of the season.

The Usk is an admirable river for fishing a wet fly in the normal three-fly cast down-and-across method. It has a good hatch of olive flies and the Blue Ruff fished in the surface film, as recommended by its creator, does well. The combination of green silk and heron herl makes for a very good olive body which is required in the early weeks of the season when many of the *Ephemeridae* family hatch

Bluebottle

PLATE 10

Hook: 12 & 14
Tying silk: Blue
Body: Peacock herl, ribbed with thick blue floss
Hackle: Honey dun

Ieuan Owen in his book *A Trout Fisherman's Saga*, about the great Dai Lewis of the Teifi, includes a pattern tied by Dai of the Bluebottle. This was not really a favourite pattern of Dai's and by the diminished standards of tying and innovation apparent in this pattern it is obvious that he had lost interest towards the end of his fishing days.

According to the account given in the book, the fly was best used after a flood, both early and late in the season. The bluebottle (*Cynomya mortuorum*) is probably the best know of the flat-wing flies, the *Diptera* family. A goodly number of newly-hatched flies from this family get blown onto the water: witness the hatches of daddy-long-legs on the rivers and lakes of Wales.

On those rich rivers where there is a plentiful food supply, members of the *Diptera* family do not assume any great importance - but on the many Welsh rivers where food is always short, all tit-bits are welcomed.

Bluebottle *(Pryce Tannatt)*

PLATE 10

Hook: 10 & 11
Tying silk: Orange
Body: Dark blue floss, ribbed with black ostrich herl
Wings: Jay's secondary quill
Hackle: Black cock

Pryce Tannatt's version of the Bluebottle proved once to be quite effective on rivers like the upper Severn, but it has lost a lot of its appeal in recent years.

Blue-Winged Olive

PLATE 10

Hook: 12 & 14
Tying silk: Green
Rib: Gold wire
Hackle: Greenish-blue hen hackle.

This pattern for *Ephemerella ignita* was devised by William Law, a renowned bailiff on the Buckland Estate on the river Usk. William Law came from Scotland where he was known as the King of the Spey. He was a great caster and an expert angler. Anglers of such stature often exercise a big influence on the angling trends in an area; and if they tie flies, then those flies can acquire a reputation not always earned. This pattern falls into that category.

The Blue-Winged Olive is a difficult fly for the angler to get to terms with and there is no indication that this pattern is any more effective than are those of David Jacques (see *The Fisherman's Fly and other Studies*, 1965).

Hook: 14
Tying silk: Dark olive
Body: Dirty olive ostrich herl wrapped with PVC
Hackle: Dark olive cock
Wing: Upright coot

In recent years the use of daylight fluorescent silk has been responsible for some very interesting body colouring. One pattern which has proved quite effective with the blue-winged olive dun on the upper Teify is as follows:

Hook: 12
Tying silk: Green
Body: Blue and lime green DFM wool very thinly applied
Hackle: Rusty blue dun

The spinner stage of the blue-winged olive is generally catered for on many Welsh rivers by the **Orange Quill**.

Hook: 14
Tying silk: Orange
Body: originally condor quill dyed hot orange, now substitutes are available
Hackle: Red cock
Wing: Starling or snipe

Bongoch *(Red Base)*

PLATE 10

Hook: 12
Tying silk: Black
Body: Black silk
Hackle: Dyed blood red
Wings: Medium dun (Starling)

Another old Welsh pattern from the Ffestiniog area. It is somewhat similar to the modern lure, Sweeny Todd, which is a jumbo version of Bongoch and used as a lure.

Bongoch is a late-season fly. Some anglers think of it as a beetle-like representation. It is recommended for use in wild and windy conditions. An old pattern, primarily designed for use on Gamallt lake in the Ffestioniog area, it has proved its value in modern times on other lakes.

Some anglers have, in the past, confused this pattern with the Cochen Las, but the hackle and the wing differ - the Bongoch being a fly of lighter hue and of more rotund form. Many anglers use it as a point fly, but it is always worth a trial on the bob. The point fly, fishing as it does, lower in the water, is the better for being thin and streamlined - while the more beetle-like flies fish better in the upper layers.

Many of the old Welsh fly patterns were meant to be fished very slowly in the water - moved in the tradition figure-of-eight retrieve. The Bongoch, dressed on bigger hooks, has produced good results when moved quite quickly on the reservoir.

Many flies, like the Bongoch, designed in Wales, up to the last decade or so, were intended to fish for brown trout. Now these flies have been put to the task of tempting rainbow trout - and brook char as well. These foreign fish - like all newcomers - have taken time to earn the respect of the locals who, experimenting with traditional Welsh flies like the Bongoch, have gradually identified their preferences.

The Bongoch, dressed very lightly, as in the original form - with just two turns of hackle, is a fair representation of a red and black buzzer pupa.

Bracken Clock

PLATE 10

Hook: 12
Tying silk: Red
Body: Red silk
Rib: Bronze peacock herl
Hackle: Cock pheasant neck feather

The quality of the cock pheasant neck hackle is often responsible for the success or failure of this pattern. It must be provided in the right size and colour. On a size 12 hook the hackle must come from about one-third of the way down the cock pheasant neck. As in the pattern Haul a Gwynt, the hackle has to stand square on the hook to get the fly to work best as a dropper. Cock pheasants vary in their shades of neck-feather colour. Some melanistic cock pheasants provide hackles in much darker hues: these are first-class.

The coch-a-bon-ddu beetles occasionally descend on Welsh lakes in great numbers and the trout quickly gorge themselves. However, after a few days, the angler will get a better response by fishing something slightly different - and this role can well be filled by the Bracken Clock which represents *Phyllopertha horitcola*. This is a fly to keep as first reserve for just such an occasion - and, as in other walks of sporting life - the reserve often scores where the first team have failed.

Brown Owl

PLATE 11

Hook: 14
Tying silk: Orange
Body: Orange silk
Head: Peacock herl
Wings: Originally, hackled with a reddish feather from the outside of a brown owl's wing. Substitutes now available of course

The Brown Owl is used to represent small sedges in late summer. The dressing is generally tied very lightly. This is a pattern that came to Wales from the north of England and gained favour with anglers in some localities. Fished around ten o'clock on a summer night it takes good quality trout as it is moved slowly in the surface film of the water.

Black Beetle

PLATE 11

Hook: 12
Tying silk: Black
Body: Ostrich herl
Wing: Black shiny crow
Hackle: Short black hen

The body of this pattern, representing *Coleopters*, is tied very full and beetle-like; the black wing is tied flat on the body. This pattern was originally the brain-child of Tom Thomas who moved to the Llangurig area from North Wales in the early twenties. He could very well have brought the pattern with him.

Butcher

PLATE 11

Hook: 10, 12 & 14
Tying silk: Black

Tail: Red ibis substitute
Body: Flat silver tinsel ribbed with silver wire
Hackle: Black hen
Wing: Blue section from mallard wing

One of the best known wet flies of all time. It has been in existence since 1838 when it was first wrought by a Mr Moon and a Mr Jewhurst from Tunbridge Wells in Kent. Mr Moon was a butcher and it could be his blue blooded apron that gave the fly its name. It is a fly that will take all season through, although it is especially effective in the early days.

It is difficult to understand why the fly was not included in a number of collections of flies used on Welsh rivers that were made during the nineteenth century.

In a bigger size the Butcher is used for sewin fishing and it has accounted for many sewin when used as a bob fly on the three wet-fly cast.

Butcher, Bloody

PLATE 11

Hook: 10, 12 & 14
Tying silk: Black
Body: Flat silver ribbed with silver wire
Hackle: Dyed red hackle
Wing: Blue section of mallard wing

A slight variation on the original Butcher is the Bloody Butcher which has a blood red hackle instead of the black one of the original.

Butcher, Kingfisher

PLATE 11

Hook: 10, 12 & 14
Tying silk: Black
Tail: Fibres from Kingfisher's wing

Hackle: Hot orange
Wing: Blue section of a mallard wing

Some anglers who fish from boats on stillwaters use another even more vividly colourful variation of the Butcher, known as the Kingfisher Butcher, a widely-used fly. Many will swear that the Kingfisher Butcher will raise fish from the darkness of the waters and that it is therefore essential as a bob fly.

Capel Celyn

PLATE 11

Hook: 12
Tying silk: Black
Tail: Two strands of mallard fibres
Rib: Copper wire
Body: Peacock quill
Hackle: Black
Wing: Jay (Blue dun)

This was widely fished in the early days on the river Celyn and hence half the name. It was fished as a point fly on a three-fly cast. Over the years the fly seems to have lost its tail, and so present day patterns tend to be tied tail-less.

The old river was drowned, as was the Capel (Chapel), when the reservoir was constructed, and so the primary element in the fly's eponymy together with its birthplace was lost. Many anglers have tried the pattern on Llyn Celyn - which can at times be a very pleasant fishery, although it is not being developed to its full potential - without exceptional success.

Many of the older anglers keep faith with their old patterns which, naturally, occupy honoured places in their fly wallets. As anglers are far more mobile today many such patterns are found being used on other distant waters. Capel Celyn has proved latterly quite effective on the tributaries of the Usk and the Wye.

Cenhinen Tony (Tony's leek)

PLATE 20

Hook: 8, 10 & 12 Longshank
Tying silk: Green
Tail: Green fluorescent floss
Rib: Gold wire
Body: Green chenille
Wing: White marabou
Hackle: Short orange cock
Head: Deer hair tied muddler fashion

In an upright position, this unusual-looking lure, devised by Tony Bevan of Llnailar, resembles the Welsh national emblem, the leek: hence the unusual name. Cenhinen Tony has survived the test of recent years and its real effectiveness is apparent towards the tail end of the season.

It really moves the fish when it is stripped back very quickly, a very tiring form of fishing. On its day a fast retrieve can provide excellent sport with rainbow trout, but, in my view, it is only a technical remove from the monotony of spinning with a fixed spool reel.

Chief

PLATE 11

Hook: 12 & 14
Tying silk: Green
Rib: Medium flat gold
Tag: Red wool
Body: Light fur from rabbit face
Hackle: Brassy dun

This fly was dressed with a very thin body, and the green tying silk was expected to show through the fur body. The rabbit fur was taken from the top layer on the face and was not to include the middle and the lower layers of fur which are very dark.

This was a pattern designed by Dai Lewis of Tregaron and is used extensively on the upper Teifi. Ieuan Owen included it in his delightful book on Dai Lewis, *A Trout Fisherman's Saga*, although it seems that it was among the flies that were marked 'Top Secret' - not for general information!

The fly was christened after a certain Chief of Police; but the pattern cannot seriously be regarded as meriting the high security classification which he endowed it. The Chief was often called upon during the 'dog days' of July, a time when most anglers eat by the sweat of their brows and fly fishing is a struggle. Any fly pattern that achieves success in difficult conditions is a far greater weapon than the average and one can understand the urge to keep quiet about it.

The Chief has proved to be more successful fished in wet form than it has as a dry fly. It is not easy to pick a good middle dropper for a three-fly cast. The bob fly, or first dropper, is often an automatic choice, as is the point fly. Doubt often exists about the middle fly. The Chief succeeds in filling this troublesome, question-mark position, and fishes well in water of light ale colour.

Tied on size 14 hooks, the Chief has done well on lakes and reservoirs. When fished on a floating line and kept in the surface film it is probably taken for a buzzer.

Chwilen Ben Glec

PLATE 11

Hook: 12
Tying silk: Black
Body: Bronze peacock herl
Tag: Silver
Hackle: Black hen
Wing: Black hen

Chwilen Ben Glec is a beetle pattern that serves as a representation of any of those black beetles (*Coleoptera*) found in the grassland adjoining lakes and rivers, which

19

inevitably get onto the water. The trout take them readily.

Some anglers have also put forward the theory that the normal Coch-a-bon-ddu pattern does not always continue to prove effective after the natural insect has been on the water for a few days. Recently, in a Welsh Championship fly fishing match held on Claerwen Reservoir, anglers fished hard for eight hours using the artificial Coch-a-bon-ddu because hordes of the naturals were about on the bank. The champion match man, however, took his winning catch of six fish with two other black patterns. Another did well with Chwilen Ben Glec - which does suggest that, under certain circumstances, black beetle approximation will serve the angler better when beetles get onto the water.

Consistent with the style of most beetle patterns, Chwilen Ben Glec is dressed with a nice full body. In windy conditions, most anglers use the pattern as a bob fly, dapped in the surface of the water. Other anglers use it as a dry fly, and in calm conditions it does take a lot of fish. One angler who, because of a physical disability leaving him unable to cast, used the Chwilen Ben Glec as the Irish do the Daddy-long-legs. This is a method that could be further developed on Welsh waters, especially as more and more of the disabled take to fishing as a hobby.

Cinnamon Sedge

PLATE 11

Hook: 12
Tying silk: Cinnamon
Body: Cinnamon turkey feather
Rib: Gold wire
Hackle: Ginger cock
Wing: Originally landrail wing feather, now use substitute
Front hackle: Ginger cock

There seems to be some doubt as to the origin of the name, some being of the opinion that it refers to the colour, while others think it is because of the smell given off by the natural insect. If it is the latter, then one can only add that it requires a very keen nose to detect it!

The cinnamon sedge (*Limnephilus lunatus*) is of medium size with yellowish cinnamon wings. The body of the female is brown and that of the male green. Fished in the evening as a dry fly it has the ability to take fish well until dark. Often it will pay the angler to move the fly and cause a wake, the wake being attractive to the fish.

Cinnamon Sedge
(J.T.H. Lane)

PLATE 11

Hook: 12
Tying silk: Golden olive
Tail: Ginger cock hackle fibres
Body: Ginger cock hackle
Wing: Ginger cock hackle fibres
Head hackle: Ginger cock

Colonel J.T.H. Lane in his book, *Lake and Loch Fishing for Trout*, 1955, suggests this pattern in which he clipped the body hackle. The clipped hackle gives the impression of a hairy body and is an excellent way of achieving a good floating fly pattern. This pattern performs well in big wave conditions on stillwaters. The advent of deer hair as body material has by now superceded the clipped hackle bodies suggested by J.T.H. Lane.

20

Cinnamon Sedge
(William Lunn)

PLATE 11

Hook: 14
Tying silk: Hot orange
Body: Swan fibres dyed a light greeny yellow
Body hackle: Buff Orpington cock hackle
Wing: Well mottled cock pheasant wing dyed cinnamon
Front hackle: One ginger and one buff Orpington cock.

William Lunn was the creator of many fly patterns while he was keeper on the river Test. This particular pattern is used occasionally on Welsh rivers but in general it is not as popular as the Lane version.

Cinnamon Sedge
(Pryce Tannatt)

PLATE 11

Hook: 9 & 10
Tying silk: Pale orange
Body: Unstripped condor quill (substitute) dyed a greenish yellow, ribbed with fine gold gimp
Wing: Rhode Island Red secondary quill
Hackle (in front of wing): Ginger cock hackle

Another first-rate pattern from Pryce Tannatt. It is a medium-sized sedge fished mainly in the dry form - although it can be quite effective on windy days used as a bob fly on a wet-fly cast. As is common with most sedges, it does best in early and late evening.

Many sedge patterns primarily designed for river fishing have transferred to stillwaters and done well in their new environment. This is true of the Cinnamon Sedge which has earned the reputation of being able to summon the trout up from the vasty deeps. On some remote Welsh mountain lakes anglers tend to fish the Cinnamon Sedge as a normal dry fly and cast along, parallel to the bank, to take trout lying close in to the bank waiting for the tit-bits that come off the land.

The following variant pattern of Cinnamon Sedge attributed to Roger Woolley is also a great favourite with Welsh anglers.

Cinnamon Sedge
(Roger Woolley)

PLATE 12

Hook: 11-13
Tying silk: Brown
Body: A strand from a cinnamon turkey tail feather
Rib: Gold wire
Body hackle: Ginger cock
Wing: Landrail wing (substitute)
Front hackle: Ginger cock

This fly was primarily designed to entice brown trout, but it has proved effective with the more commonly stocked rainbows in stillwaters. It is also gaining its place as a grayling fly on the river Dee. It is probably most effective when used as a dry fly in the late evening. A good quality hackle allows the pattern to be fished in the surface film and the angler, by jerking the rod tip, makes the fly skit across the surface - thus emulating the action of a sedge caught in the surface film of the water.

Coachman

PLATE 12

Hook: 12 & 14
Tying silk: Brown
Body: Peacock herl

Hackle: Ginger cock or hen
Wing: White swan or hen

The Coachman is one of the best known of all artificial fancy flies, yet many anglers will not give it box-room. Any pattern that has been existence for over a hundred and fifty years, and has produced as many variants, has somehow to be both favoured and effective. It bears no resemblance to any known living insect and therefore must be classed as a fancy fly, holding some mysterious general appeal for the trout.

Only a few river anglers in Wales now use the Coachman, when it can, especially in late Spring and Summer, do service as a dry fly in its hackle form in the late evening. The white wing aids visibility on dark evenings, or when fishing against the sun-set.

The Coachman now seems to have more followers on the stillwaters where many anglers, disliking the pure white wing of bought varieties, immediately set about removing its 'whiter than whiteness'. This has led to the adoption, now pretty widespread, of the so-called 'Lead-Winged Coachman'. Some also use the Coachman in the smaller sizes when trout are 'smutting' and reluctant to look at more conventional flies.

In the early fifties, interesting to look back on, the Coachman was much used for sewin fishing, the white wing being held in high esteem. Fashions change, and the Coachman went out when the 'new wave' sewin flies came on the scene in the early sixties. Very few sewin anglers use it today.

Some confusion exists about the origin of this pattern. A Tom Bosworth who acted as a coachman to George IV and William IV has been credited as its inventor - although a certain John Hughes, a man of Kent who fished the river Cray, is also said to have first dressed the fly from bits and pieces. He also has claims to the honour. So simple is the pattern that undoubtedly quite a number of people 'invented' it.

Coachman, Lead-winged

PLATE 12

Hook: 12
Tying silk: Brown
Body: Peacock herl
Hackle: Ginger cock
Wing: Blue dun jay wing

This was not, until its recent use on stillwaters, quite so well-known as the ordinary Coachman, despite the fact that, under certain conditions, it does better because of its more subdued wing. There is no doubt that the contrast of a vivid, white wing on a sober body does, under certain light conditions, put the fish off.

Coachman, Royal

PLATE 12

Hook: 12
Tying silk: Brown
Body: Peacock herl with a centre portion of bright red floss
Hackle: Ginger cock
Wing: White swan, duck or hen

This Americanisation of the original pattern is a very gaudy version, favoured by rainbow trout in light and water conditions seldom found in the British Isles. It is very occasionally used on the rivers in Wales.

Cob, Brecon

PLATE 12

Hook: 12
Tying silk: Claret
Rib: Gold wire
Body: Dark red silk or seal's fur

Hackle: Dark partridge hackle
Wing: Hen pheasant wing

In the Brecon anglers refer to the March Brown as the Cob and they have the Cob made up in a number of different colours. The notes relating to the March brown insect (*Rithrogena haarupi*) are applicable here.

Cob, Orange

PLATE 12

Hook: 12
Tying silk: Orange
Rib: Gold wire
Body: Orange floss
Hackle: Dark brown partridge
Wing: Hen pheasant

The Orange Cob is not quite so widely known and therefore - unlike its yellow cousin (see below) - is not so much used on the river Usk. Yet, like many other little-known patterns, it can have its day.

Cob, Yellow

PLATE 12

Hook: 12
Tying silk: Yellow
Rib: Gold wire
Body: Yellow seal's fur
Hackle: Dark partridge
Wing: Hen pheasant

Doyen of Brecon fly fishers, Leslie Peters, who has fished the river Usk at Brecon for the last fifty years, has great faith in his Yellow Cob, an early season fly.

Coch-a-bon-ddu

PLATE 12

Hook: 12 & 14
Tying silk: Crimson
Body: Two strands of bronze peacock herl tied full
Hackle: Coch-a-bon-ddu.

In centuries past the highlands of Wales were covered in carpets of heather, and in June and July beetles (*Phyllopertha horticola*) would descend from on high onto the rivers and lakes in great numbers, providing a spread of banquet proportions for the fish. The trout feasted for days on these beetles, and the fly known as the Coch-a-bon-ddu was used by anglers to catch them.

In recent years the heather has been replaced by sinister armies of green coniferous trees which sustain practically no insect life. Certain doubts existed originally about the identity of this beetle, with some anglers confusing it with the Marlow buzz, bracken clock, the shorn fly and the mini cockchafer.

The coch-a-bon-ddu beetle has a reddish brown body with a dark peacock green thorax and red-black legs. The Coch-a-bon-ddu, too, has the unique distinction of being the most mis-spelt fly name. Seldom is it correctly spelt - in any book or article - because its Welsh ancestry is either forgotten or mistaken for the Gaelic. Even Courtney Williams in his estimable *A Dictionary of Trout Flies*, makes a hash of it, and he had less excuse than many!

Expert etymologists (not entomologists!) of the calibre of Bedwyr Lewis-Jones and the late Jac L. Williams, affirm that the term coch-a-bon-ddu in Welsh is descriptive of an insect which is red with a black base. The only other spelling admissible would be coch-a-bonddu which would be about as elegant as 'red-and-black base' in English!

The hackle is tied rather heavily. Some add a gold tag to the dressing although this did not appear on the original. Others rib the body with gold wire and it is probably true to say that the ribbing is present as much to protect the herls as anything. A recent trend is to use red fluorescent filaments for the ribbing.

It would certainly be wrong to think the Coch-a-bon-ddu artificial fly is only effective when the natural is about. On a cold March day in 1965 the late Evan Owen of Ynysbwl took twelve beauties on the Claerwen reservoir with 'the Cocky' as he called it. The dozen fell to the Coch-a-bon-ddu as it was bobbed along the surface, proving how effective it ca be as a bob fly.

George Agar Hansard in 1834 refers to the Drop Fly, as a dropper tied onto the cast by means of a hog's bristle! The pattern he gives of the Drop Fly is not dissimilar to the Coch-a-bon-ddu. Reference to George Scotcher's book *The Fly Fisher's Legacy* suggests the origin at least of the practice of fishing the Coch-a-bon-ddu on the bob.

The Coch-a-bon-ddu is also often used as a dry fly, especially on water thinning down after a flood. Here, in this guise, it would be wrong to think of it as a specific copy of a particular insect - but rather as a general all-rounder to fish during the summer months.

There is a tendency in Wales to fish trout flies tied on bigger hooks to catch sewin. A big bushy Coch-a-bon-ddu tied on a number six or eight hook has been the downfall of many an over-sanguine sewin. On a moonlight night in July, Cecil Jones of Llandysul took half a dozen sewin on a Coch-a-bon-ddu fished in the classical dry fly manner up-river from the Oak Pool. Most of the club anglers fished the traditional sewin wet fly method that same night and were fishless.

Cochen-las

PLATE 12

Hook: 12 & 14
Tying silk: Black
Body: Black floss
Hackle: Coch-a-bon-ddu or black centre with single red outers
Wing: Dark dun, coot

A copy of the Cochen-las was received from the late Ned Hughes who, in the late fifties, was a celebrity among Rhayader anglers. The hackle on that specimen was Coch-a-bon-ddu; and Monty Powell, also from Rhayader, produced similar examples. Recently, however, a number of so-called Cochen-las have appeared where the hackle used is one with a black centre and with blood-red outers. This is obviously a badger hackle dipped in blood-red dye. Another instance seen lately supported a hackle of black-orange which also is reputed to work well. Obviously, then there are instances like this when it is not so easy to determine the authentic dressing of a vernacular fly where local opinion differs so sharply over its specification. The Ned Hughes version has always been assumed by most to be the authentic Cochen-las: though now we have to recognise that hackles with red tips are proving successful.

As far as the name Cochen-las is concerned, it simply means 'red-blue-one'. The 'las' is a mutation of the Welsh word 'glas' which means the colour blue (and sometimes green). It has nothing to do with the Scottish word 'lass' (double 'S') meaning a girl - though, curiously, there is a girl skulking somewhere in the word Cochen, for it means a red-head and, as 'blonde' seldom conjures a male, so the cochen is necessarily female - not impossibly a 'lass'! So Cochen-las, if you like, 'a blue red-head'. A useful fly on Claerwen (and all mountain lakes with wild brown trout) and on the upper reaches of the Wye around Rhayader where she spent her early days: since when she has grown up in beauty, stature and fascination, a winsome companion to mountain lakes.

Coch-yn-las

PLATE 12

Hook: 14 & 15
Tying silk: Purple
Body: Strand from brown turkey tail dyed purple
Hackle: Dark rusty dun cock
Wings: Water hen secondary quill

Pryce Tannatt confused many people with the name that he gave this pattern because they mixed it with the Cochen-las. The 'red-in-blue' of the nomenclature here clearly means a mixture of pigmentation resulting in purple (see also Snipe & Purple and Usk Purple).

This Coch-yn-las has proved to be a good trout and grayling pattern, used primarily in the early days of the season and again in September when many of the early season flies come back into their own. It became very popular on the Irfon, a tributary of the Wye, and on the Ceiriog. The Coch-yn-las also gained some success on stillwaters, like Claerwen, although there is some doubt as to whether all anglers questioned knew the difference between the two patterns. It could be that the success gained by one was being attributed to the other.

Cog (Sepia Dun)

PLATE 12

Hook: 12
Tying silk: Purple
Rib: Thin gold wire
Body: Chocolate coloured silk
Hackle: Ginger cock
Wing: Brown mallard, not too brown

This fly, used quite extensively in the Ffestiniog area of North Wales, is recognised as the fly to use when the sepia dun (*Leptophlebia marginata*) is in evidence. Quite some importance is attached to the position that the fly should occupy on the cast and the Cog is used 'next to hand' (Nesaf at law) or on the bob.

Cogyn Now'r Allt

PLATE 13

Hook: 12
Tying silk: Black
Tail: Ginger fibres
Rib: Silver wire
Body: Rear half yellow silk. Front half blue silk
Hackle: Black hen
Wing: Light blue dun

Now'r Allt, 'Now (Noah?) of the woods' was one of those human curiosities, half hermit, wild man of the woods, known in Wales as 'dyn hysbys' (man with knowledge), a soothsayer. It was said that he even talked to the fish, and this, his version of the Cog is particularly interesting as it is in direct contact with angling wizardry.

The sepia dun has a very dark body and dark wings. It has three tails which generally spread well out. It is the first of the 'upwing' flies to appear and they generally show during the warmest part of the day. Many anglers rely on the Pheasant Tail pattern to serve them on the lake when the sepia dun is hatching, but the Blaenau Ffestiniog pattern, Cog, being darker, can often be more effective. Recently, some Welsh anglers have been using copper wire under the dressing of the Cog in order to get the pattern to fish deeper in the water. This is worth trying.

PLATE 1
Alexandra, Blackie, Allrounder
Blue Black & Silver (variant), Brown Bomber, Blue Black & Silver Squirrel
Brown & Yellow Mole, Bomber, Closs Special
Conway Badger, Conway Red
Cooke's Bogey

PLATE 2
Dai Ben, Dovey Black & Orange, Doctor's Special
Yellow Bumble, Dovey Bumble, Claret Bumble
Fiery Brown Bumble
Earley's Fancy (No.1), Earley's Fancy (No.2)
White Owl, Polly Perkins

Concoction

PLATE 13

Hook: 8 & 10
Tying silk: Green
Rib: Gold wire
Body: Rear half green seal's fur. Front half red seal's fur
Wing: Light hen pheasant wing or owl
Hackle: Ginger

This fly is a variation of the old Irish pattern, Green Peter, with red seal's fur added to the body. Arthur Owen, highly respected among anglers on the Trawsfynydd fishery, devised this pattern when on a visit to Chew Valley for an International fly fishing match.

Arthur, as captain of the Welsh team, produced some astounding catches with this pattern. It has proved its value on stillwaters in Wales - like Clywedog and Brenig - in addition to its home waters of Trawsfynydd.

It is generally fished on the bob, but such is the faith that some anglers have in it that they also, at the same time, place it on the point. One angler was known to have four on his cast on one particular day on Trawsfynydd. There's no need to ask what fly was proving effective that day!

Cord

PLATE 13

Hook: 12 & 14
Tying silk: yellow
Body: Hessian sack pickings
Hackle: Blue andalusian

Designed by Ernest Lewis of Glynneath who was employed on the Rheola Estate.

The Cord is used on the Neath after the water has started to warm up.

Ernie placed great importance on the blue Andalusian hackle. The blue hackle is held in high esteem in South Wales and some anglers care little for the body of the fly as long as the quality and colour of the hackle is correct.

The Cord has travelled well and has been successful on sections of the upper Severn. It would appear that it is especially effective when the olives hatch at the beginning of the season.

Corixa

PLATE 25

Hook: 12
Tying silk: White
Rib: Brown cotton
Body: Cream floss dressed full
Wing case: A strip of dark brown wing fibre tied in at the tail and brought over the back and then tied in at the head
Legs: Cream hen hackle tied in under the head

The corixa, or water beetle, is a common item of food for trout in the late season. It is generally found near weed beds and is fairly active as it moves to the surface to get a supply of air. On taking in this fresh supply of oxygen the corixa sinks down with a glistening air bubble between its wing and body.

The recognised method of fishing it is to incorporate some lead wire in the dressing, thus ensuring that it sinks quickly. Used on a long leader with a floating line, the angler casts it out near to the weeds and lets it sink. It is then retrieved in short jerks.

Corixa (Tony Brett)

PLATE 25

Hook: 12, 14 & 16
Tying silk: Yellow, waxed
Body: Lime green wool
Tag: Three turns silver thread
Rib: Silver wire

Back: Feathers from magpie tail
Paddles: Large lime green goose biots
Head: Large black varnished eyes

Tony Brett and his wife Felicity are both very keen fishers and they will often be found fishing one or other of the Cardiff reservoirs.

Tony's Corixa can be fished either low in the water or in the higher levels. It is advisable to add some lead wire to the dressing if it is intended to fish the corixa deep. Tony, being an excellent caster, puts his Corixa well out into the reservoir and then works it back in a series of sink-and-draw movements - which emulates the movement of the natural.

Cowdung

PLATE 13

Hook: 12 & 14
Tying silk: Brown
Body: Dirty yellow wool, pinch of brown
Hackle: Pale ginger
Wing: Woodcock

A variation of an old pattern created by Alfred Ronalds to imitate the cowdung fly (*Scatophago stercoraria*) when being blown onto the river. In the early forties it was a pattern much used as a wet fly and is similar to the Woodcock & Yellow. Latterly, it has been used more in its dry form, on the smaller rivers, during low water conditions.

Some fly-dressers do not put a wing on the dry version of the Cowdung fly. In addition to the normal pale ginger hackle they add a winging of cree feather which gives a sparkle to the fly. Scotcher used golden plover, or alternatively, corncrake, starling or a pale ginger hackle. Clearly, exactness of imitation was not of high importance.

Crane Fly (Daddy-long-legs)

PLATE 13

Hook: 10, 11, & 12
Tying silk: Pale orange
Body: Stripped herl from moon peacock feather.
Wings: Rolled and split woodcock secondary quill
Hackles: Rusty dun cock

The old dressing of Pryce Tannatt (above) is now seldom used, despite being extremely effective two decades ago. There has of late been a great upsurge in the interest shown in Crane flies (*Tipulidae*), due to the success they have been giving anglers on the big stillwaters. Consequently, the old art of dapping has shown something of a revival.

Although the first of the crane flies will be seen in April, it is in summer and the autumn that they really summon the trout onto the surface of the water. There exists some confusion as to how the Crane Fly is best fished. Some tend to move it in the surface of the water, others advocate leaving it motionless on the water - or dapping.

The following modern pattern is to be fished as a dry fly and left to lie on the water without movement:

Hook: 10
Tying silk: Brown
Body: Green or brown herl or deer hair
Legs: 6 cock pheasant centre tail fibres, knotted
Wings: Cree hackle points
Hackle: Ginger cock

Crawshay's Olive

PLATE 13

Hook: 12
Tying silk: Yellow
Tail: Honey dun fibres

Body: Mole fur
Rib: Yellow silk (prominent)
Hackle: Honey dun
Wing: Coot or starling

This fly has the look of being very successful, and it is. It is rather a delicate pattern with an overall colour of olive dun; the yellow silk, the honey dun hackle and the mole fur forming the effective colour pattern. It is one of those special fly patterns that inspires confidence.

When fished on a fine leader in the runs and glides of the river Usk, the Crawshay's Olive is taken for a member of the olive family in one stage or other of its development. Despite its overall delicate dun shade it is an effective evening pattern, fished just under the surface of the water. It is particularly successful on the Glannusk and Crawshay estate, from which it originates.

Cream

PLATE 13

Hook: 12
Tying silk: Yellow
Body: The fur of a Teddy Bear
Hackle: Light blue dun hen

This is a wet pattern devised by Ernest Lewis of Glyn Neath. His very original fly patterns are still much valued especially on the river Neath. They are also proving their ability to take fish on the Ystradfellte Reservoir, which is managed by the anglers of Glyn Neath.

This pattern is tied using a fairly pale blue dun hackle. The shade of the hackle is important, and some anglers recommend that only the 'butt' be used.

Dafydd Lloyd

PLATE 13

Hook: 8 & 10
Tying silk: Yellow
Rib: Flat gold tinsel
Body: A fawny yellow floss
Hackle: Ginger cock
Wing: Bronze mallard

Most of the sedge patterns devised in North Wales are of a dark hue and this particular one seems to be in sharp contrast to the general trend. It is often used in conjunction with a dark patter, such as Y Rhwyfwr Mawr Cochddu thereby offering the best of both ends of the colour spectrum to the trout.

Despite giving this pattern extensive trials on some waters in other parts of Wales, it has not registered much success.

The Dafydd Lloyd pattern works well on Clywedog Reservoir in the evenings and it proves to be most attractive when fished quickly just under the surface. Some anglers believe that it does well when the 'biga moth' hatches on the reservoir. This curious and unique insect has a yellow body, brown legs and brown wings. It descends from the forest in June, throughout the day, and when it lands on the water the trout unanimously vote for it with their mouths.

Devonshire Doctor

PLATE 13

Hook: 12
Tying silk: Black
Rib: Flat gold
Body: Black floss or seal's fur
Hackle: Coch-a-bon-ddu

The Welsh version of this fly is associated with North Wales: **Pluen Cochddu ar gorff du** (Coch-a-bon-ddu feather on black body).

PLATE 3
Fiery Brown, Wasp Fly, Grey Goose
Harry Tom, Kingsmill, Huw Nain
Lewi's Killer, Mallard & Silver
Marchog Coch
Marchog Glas

This wet fly is used in the normal down-and-across method on rivers. It is most effective as a lightly dressed point fly and has most success towards the tail-end of the season. The Teifi Terror, a sewin pattern, is very similar to the Devonshire Doctor.

Diawl Bach

PLATE 13

Hook: 12
Tying silk: Black
Tail: Brown fibres
Body: Peacock herl
Legs: Dark brown hen.

A 'Mr Evans from Cardiff' is attributed with the invention of this pattern and, it would appear, that he used to fish the Chew fishery where, in the evenings especially. He would take many trout with it. The Diawl Bach appears to be nymph-like, though it is difficult to conceive what item of food the trout take it for. The pattern is held in high esteem by notable Chew anglers like John Braithwaite and Steve Pope.

Dog Nobbler (black)

PLATE 21

Hook: 6, 8 & 10 Long shank
Tying silk: Black
Tail: Bunch of black marabou
Body: Black chenille
Head: Lead shot or bead fixed with glue

This is a very popular pattern on big reservoirs. It is tied in all colours and trout seem to vary in their colour preference from day to day, so it is advisable to carry a selection of different colours.

As with most lures, the speed of retrieve is important and should be varied. In high summer when the fish are really difficult, an orange or a yellow Nobbler stripped as fast as the angler possibly can will sometimes get the fish to take. The slow retrieve under such conditions is not productive.

The principle of attaching a hackle to the mid and tail section of the fly is certainly not new and the sewin pattern, Night Heron, tied by Lewi Davies of Llandeilo in the 1940s, used the same technique. Nobblers have been know to score some success with sewin.

Drudwy Corff Du
(Starling wing on black body)

PLATE 13

Hook: 12
Tying silk: Black
Tail: Blue dun hackle fibres
Rib: Flat silver
Body: Black silk
Wing: Starling wing

A fly used for fishing the small mountain lakes and was considered to be something of a 'secret' pattern. The late J.O. Jones of Llanrwst was the first to publicise it in his contribution to John Veniard's book *A Further Guide to Fly Dressing*. 'J.O.' used it to good effect on Loch Leven and, when tied in the smaller sizes, especially when dressed very lightly - as was customary with many of the North Wales fly dressers - it made an excellent representation of the black midge pupa.

It has performed as a useful sewin fly on the upper reaches of the river Aeron.

Dunkeld

PLATE 13

Hook: 8, 10 & 12
Tying silk: Orange
Tail: Golden pheasant toppings
Body: Flat gold tinsel, ribbed with gold wire

Hackle: Hot orange cock
Wing: Bronze mallard
Cheeks: Two small jungle cock 'eyes' (or substitutes)

This is one of the best flies in current use on Welsh reservoirs. There is hardly one reservoir on which this pattern does not figure in the top half dozen favourite flies. It is an attractor fly with high visibility qualities and is especially good when used on a sunken line and retrieved quickly.

One effective variation on the original pattern has been the use of a green fluorescent tail. Designed for Scottish brown trout, this fly is best known in Wales for its powers with rainbow trout in stillwater. It is also a pattern for sewin - especially just following a flood when the water still contains traces of colour. Try fishing it in tandem form.

Du'r Fran (Crow's Black)

PLATE 13

Hook: 13
Tying silk: Black
Rib: Thin gold wire
Body: Black silk
Hackle: Dyed blood red
Wing: Dark dun (crow wing)

Another black pattern from Ffestiniog. When dressed thinly this is an ideal point fly.

The use of a blood-red hackle was much in evidence on many Welsh rivers about fifty years ago. The Welsh word used to describe this hackle was 'fflambo' and at one time practically every area had a Fflambo pattern using 'Flambo legs'. The Du'r Fran with its red hackle, is very effective on the rivers and lakes of North Wales.

Early Brown

PLATE 13

Hook: 12 & 13
Tying silk: Hot orange
Body: Hare's ear dubbed thinly on tying silk
Hackle: Under covert feather from a woodcock wing

This pattern appeared in the Pryce-Tannatt collection and it has proved to be an effective pattern when the natural (*Protonemura meyeri*) is about in the early days of the season. The early brown is a minor member of the *Perlidae* family, a smaller member of the order of stoneflies.

The Early Brown is best fished as a middle fly on a three-fly cast and has proved to be effective on fine days in early Spring on the Usk and Teifi.

Other patterns that are also effective, fished when the early brown is about, are Brown Owl and Winter Brown.

Edmondson's Welsh Fly

PLATE 14

Hook: 10
Tying silk: Yellow
Body: Dirty yellow mohair, tipped at tail with gold tinsel
Hackle: Furnace
Wing: Woodcock's wing

Edmondson, a tackle dealer living in Liverpool, invented this fly which was used on North Wales lakes.

Primarily a stillwater fly, although some claim has been made for it as a late-season river fly, there is no doubt that it once enjoyed considerable status. Today this has diminished considerably. Yet Edmondson's Welsh Fly can still have its day on places like Claerwen and Clywedog.

PLATE 4
Old Favourite, Night Heron
Pry Copyn, Mouse,
Rancid Racoon, Red Mackerel, Silver Grey
Tom Tom, Teifi Terror, Torby Coch
Harries' Sedge, Water Rat & Red
Towy Topper, Twm Twll, Wil Harry's Green Woodcock

PLATE 5
Worm Fly, Yellow Plasterer
Treble Chance, Moc's Beauty
Evening Serenade, Midnight Magic, Pussy Galore
Moc's Bumble, Princess Di, Fiery Jack
Moc's Cert

Egarych Cochddu
(Corncrake wing on black-red body)

PLATE 13

Hook: 10
Tying silk: Brown
Rib: Gold wire
Body: Wool from black ram's scrotum
Hackle: Brown partridge
Wing: Originally corncrake (now sandy coloured hen)

The Corncrake patterns are included for historical interest and not as an encouragement for enthusiastic tyros. The corncrake has been driven to near extinction by modern farming methods. The wing of this pattern is now tied with an ordinary hen wing feather which in any case makes a better winging material.

This pattern is especially effective when the small brown sedge is about and will take fish when fished either wet or dry.

Egarych Corff Llygoden Ddwr (Corncrake wing with water rat body)

PLATE 13

Hook: 10
Tying silk: Brown
Rib: Gold wire
Body: Fur from water rat
Hackle: Ginger cock (palmered)
Wing: Originally corncrake (use starling substitute)

An important pattern for the September fisher when the little red sedge is about.

Egarych Dyfrgi
(Corncrake wing on otter body)

PLATE 13

Hook: 10
Tying silk: Brown
Rib: Gold wire
Body: Whitish fur of otter (now use rabbit).
Hackle: Ginger
Wing: Corncrake (now use sandy hen)

Today rabbit skin provides all the fur necessary for this dressing. The light-coloured body is especially attractive to trout when used in the evening.

Egarych Clust Sgwarnog
(Corncrake wing on hare's body)

PLATE 13

Hook: 10
Tying silk: Brown
Rib: Gold wire
Body: Hare's ear fur
Hackle: Ginger cock
Wing: Originally corncrake (now use sandy hen)

This pattern is equally at home on river and stillwater. It represents the little brown sedge and takes fish during the day as well as in the evening. The wings, when used in its wet form, must slope back - flat over body. If used dry, they can be put at a more upright angle and split into two separate wings.

Egarych Corff Paun
(Corncrake on peacock herl)

PLATE 13

Hook: 10
Tying silk: Brown
Rib: Gold wire
Body: Peacock herl
Hackle: Ginger
Wing: Corncrake (now use sandy hen)

Herl makes an ideal bulky body, characteristic of the Sedge and Beetle patterns.

Emyr's Fancy

Hook: 12
Tying silk: Black
Rib: Gold wire
Body: Black seal's fur
Thorax: A mixture of fiery brown, green and black seal's fur

This nymph was developed on the Clywedog fishery by Emyr Lloyd, a bailiff employed by the Welsh Water Authority. During the early season it is fished deep with a little copper wire being added under the dressing to achieve a quick-sinking effect. As the water warms up in late spring and summer the nymph is fished closer to the surface.

Clywedog is stocked with rainbow as well as with brown trout. In most Welsh fisheries the rainbow does not acquire that silvery sheen which makes it such a handsome trout. It does so in Clywedog - and it moves well to nymphs fished near the surface.

Eric's Beetle

PLATE 9

Hook: 8
Tying silk: Yellow
Body: Bronze peacock herl over yellow wool with some yellow showing at tail
Hackle: Two turns of black hen

The beetle family is important to the upland angler. Eric Horsfall Turner spent a lot of time fishing the uplands of the Severn valley. It is fitting to record this pattern in memory of that grand old angler.

February Red

PLATE 14

Hook: 12, 14
Tying silk: Red
Rib: Gold wire
Body: Red wool
Hackle: Dark brown partridge

February red is a member of the ubiquitous order of stoneflies which provide that essential early bite for Spring trout in some areas. Of all the stoneflies, the February red (*Taeniopteryx nebulosa*) is the most localised in distribution, although it is very significant, where it does appear.

On the upper Teifi it shows in considerable numbers, and the above pattern has been in use for decades in the Tregaron area.

This pattern is also used to good effect when the Early brown (*Protonemura meyeri*) is in evidence. The Early brown is similar in colour to the February red, but its wings tend to have more of a greyish tint rather than a brownish one.

Even as late as the thirties and forties anglers in the upper Teifi tended to be rather conservative in their choice of wet flies. Into March and early April the

February Red was always on the cast, fished in the middle position on a three-fly cast.

Felan Fach
(Little Yellow One)

PLATE 14

Hook: 14
Tying silk: Yellow
Tail: Golden pheasant tippets
Body: Gold tinsel
Hackle: Light ginger hen
Wing: Snipe speckled feather

In bright sunlight, the odd fish will just cruise along taking flies near the surface and the Felan Fach is designed to deceive and have him.

Designed by Gwilym Hughes of Wrexham. Felan Fach has proved its value on lakes like Trawsfynydd, Brenig and Alaw. It is more effective with rainbow trout than with the browns. The Felan Fach demands good presentation and it will then help the angler to get a trout under harsh light conditions.

Fflambo

PLATE 14

Hook: 10
Tying silk: Black
Body: Claret seal's fur or wool
Rib: Gold wire
Hackle: Claret hackle
Wing: Bronze mallard

This pattern has a good reputation as a sedge fly in North Wales and is considered by many anglers to be the best fly to use for their night fishing.

The dressing is applied rather heavily, and is totally out of character with many of the old fly dressings from the same area. The seal's fur body is made quite thick - with the gold rib being put on tight to emphasise the segmentation. The claret hackle should have six to eight turns and the mallard wing rolled to form a heavy wing that extends well over the bend of the hook.

Sedges played an important part in the angling lives of many of the quarrymen of North Wales. Their's was a hard life, the hours of work often extending from dawn until dusk. Their angling activity was often necessarily limited to the hours of darkness. The Rhwyfwyr (Sedges) thus assumed far greater importance for them than they would have for the so-called 'gentlemen anglers'. The Fflambo is a night pattern which probably suggests the grouse wing sedge (*Mystacides longicornis*).

Francis' Fly

PLATE 14

Hook: 12 & 10
Tying silk: Red
Body: Copper coloured peacock herl ribbed distinctly with copper red silk
Hackle: Medium blue dun
Wings: Two hackle points of a grizzly blue dun cock's hackle set well up

This is an old fly which was first mentioned in *The Angler's Register* in 1858, by Francis Francis, its creator. He gave this fly extensive trials in Wales and was convinced that it was a truly great fly. Courtney Williams for one does not agree with Francis Francis. The claims for it as a sewin fly are also hard to substantiate. It is worth keeping the pattern handy, as was proved on Ystradfellte reservoir recently. Rainbow trout which had been very dour all morning took a Francis Fly with confidence on the point of a two-fly cast.

PLATE 6
Black Doctor, Blue Doctor
Silver Doctor, Conway Blue
Dwyryd Red & Yellow, Haslam
Irt Fly

Grannom

PLATE 14

Hook: 12
Tying silk: Green
Body: Mole fur dyed in picric acid
Hackle: Two biscuit coloured partridge hackles.

This pattern was evolved by Vicar Powell after he had discussed the grannom problem with Dai Lewis. The partridge feathers for the hackle, which must be of the right colour, are found mid-way between the back and neck. The two hackles are tied in back-to-back. Many anglers have been disappointed with this pattern, but this is most probably the result of it being fished incorrectly. Vicar Powell did not fish his Grannom as a dry fly, but rather in the surface film.

On the upper Teifi the grannom (*Brachycentrus subnubilis*) starts hatching between the fifteenth and the twentieth of April. It will then hatch spasmodically until the seventh of May.

The female grannom is slightly larger than the male and she has a greenish hue on the last few segments of her body. Many anglers think that trout only go for the female grannom and that they ignore the males. This is not conclusively proven - but most successful dressings do use green material.

Grannom, Halford's

PLATE 14

Hook: 13
Tying silk: Green
Body: Green floss silk ribbed with green dyed peacock quill
Hackle: Rusty dun.

Gravel Bed (Rev. Powell)

PLATE 14

Hook: 13 & 14
Tying silk: Yellow
Body: Blue rabbit under pelt
Hackle: Blue dun with light ginger in front

This pattern is easy. The body is tied rather thinly with the yellow silk just showing in the dubbed blue body. The blue dun hackle is tied behind the ginger one.

Found in abundance on Welsh rivers, the gravel bed (*Hexatoma fuscipennis*) has a dark body with six long olive legs and two slate-coloured wings that lie flat along the back. Though it is a member of *Tipulidae*, it is not unlike members of the crane fly family. It is not generally seen on Welsh rivers before early May. The insect is amphibious and its metamorphosis takes place on dry land. As it moves about on the surface of the water it can occasion the trout to feed for long spells and, on some rivers, it is regarded as the 'poor man's Mayfly'. There are a good number of artificial patterns for the gravel bed - but the one received by the author from Rev Edward Powell (as a token of appreciation for a small present of coch-a-bon-ddu hackles) is probably the best. The Rev Gentleman himself even admitted to pride in this above all his many patterns.

Gravel Bed (Alfred Ronalds)

PLATE 14

Hook: 13
Tying silk: Lead-coloured
Body: Lead coloured silk
Hackle: A long black cock, two turns only
Wing: Under coverts of woodcock wing

Alfred Ronalds fished this pattern during hot bright weather and often used it when other patterns had failed.

Gravel Bed
(Pryce Tannatt)

PLATE 14

Hook: 12 & 13
Tying silk: Grey wool
Body: Cigar-ash coloured wool, wound on and then lightly varnished with diluted Durafix
Hackle: Two turns of natural black cock hackle, an over-sized hackle with a grey-ish brown feather from a partridge

Gravel Bed (variant)

PLATE 14

Hook: 13 & 14
Tying silk: Purple
Body: Peacock quill with purple silk showing at tail
Hackle: Black cock

A friend who confines all his fishing to the dry fly on the rivers Dee and Severn received this wingless pattern from a relation in Scotland. His confidence in the pattern is well justified. It works well as a wet fly too.

Green Peter

PLATE 14

Hook: 10 & 12
Tying silk: Green
Rib: Gold Wire
Body: Green seal's fur
Wing: Hen pheasant
Hackle: Ginger

This Irish fly has enjoyed considerable success on Welsh stillwaters as a bob fly. The correct shade of seal's fur for the body is a warm olive green, dressed rather bulkily. The ginger hackle is often palmered down the body as is the custom with many Irish fly dressers.

Greenwell's Glory

PLATES 14 & 23

Hook: 12 & 14
Tying silk: Yellow
Rib: Gold wire
Hackle: Coch-a-bon-ddu
Wing: Hen blackbird

Cannon William Greenwell of Durham achieved piscatorial immortality when he invented this pattern. The first example was tied up for him by James Wright, a well known fly dresser living in Sprouston on the Tweed.

Such is the versatility of the pattern that it can serve not only as a river fly for trout - but as a reservoir and lake pattern - and also, when dressed on hooks 8 and 10, it takes sewin in daylight. A general all-round pattern which suggests a whole range of flies - mainly from the olive family.

Greenwell, Dai's

PLATE 14

Hook: 13
Tying silk: Green
Rib: Gold wire
Tail: Golden pheasant tippets
Body: Green silk
Hackle: Greenwell

This fly is rather uncharacteristic of Dai Lewis's repertoire in that it is colourful. Most of Dai's flies, as is well known, were inclined to be somewhat sombre. Dai considered his Greewell best for the point position on a three-fly cast.

41

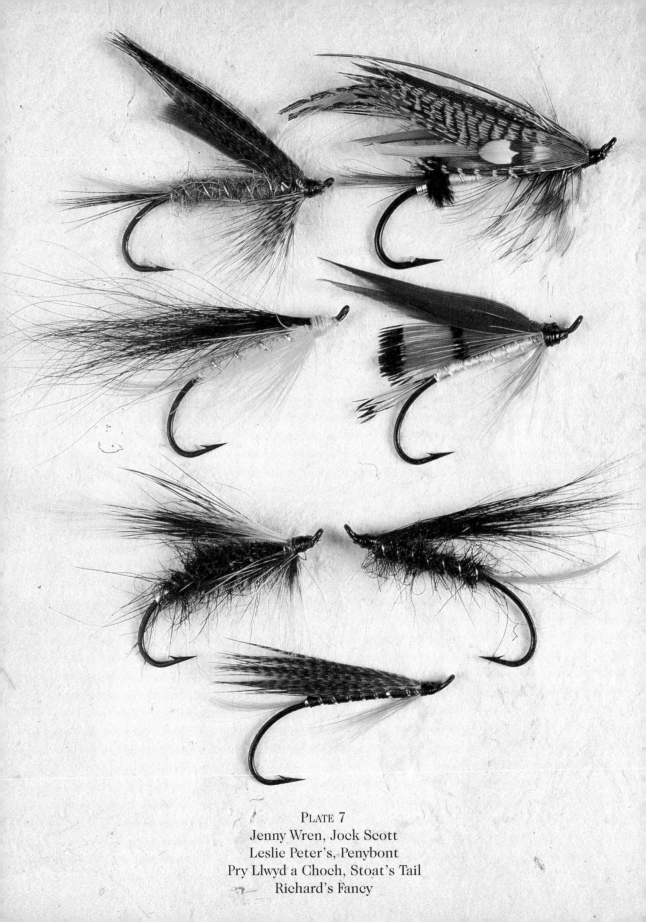

PLATE 7
Jenny Wren, Jock Scott
Leslie Peter's, Penybont
Pry Llwyd a Choch, Stoat's Tail
Richard's Fancy

PLATE 8
Thunder & Lightning, Twrci Coch
Twrci Du, Welsh Shrimp Fly
Welsh Shrimp Fly (variant), Usk Grub
Wil Harry

It is still used by many local anglers on the upper Teifi and on its day does extremely well. Dai himself on one memorable day took seventeen sewin, fishing the top reaches of the Camddwr - some six miles from Tregaron - all on a big version of his Greenwell.

Grenadier

PLATE 14

Hook: 12
Tying silk: Brown
Rib: Gold wire
Body: Hot orange seal's fur
Hackle: Two turns of ginger hackle

The Grenadier, has proved effective on many Welsh Reservoirs. Cast it well out on a floating line and then strip it back rather quickly. This method seems to attract trout which are cruising just under the surface. Some dressers like to palmer the hackle in order to create more surface disturbance when fishing the fly in this quick-retrieve manner. It bears a striking relationship to the Teifi Pools Sedge.

Grouse & Claret

PLATE 15

Hook: 12 & 10
Tying silk: Claret
Tail: Golden pheasant tippets
Rib: Gold wire
Body: Claret seal's fur
Hackle: Ginger
Wing: Mottled feather from a grouse's tail

This pattern is a stillwater pattern. The Grouse & Claret, the most popular of the Grouse series in Wales, is regarded by many as a good substitute for the Mallard & Claret. In recent years some anglers have tended to add a pinch of black seal's fur to the normal Mallard & Claret body in an attempt to darken the pattern and use a grouse wing to try to achieve this darkening of the pattern.

Grouse & Green

PLATE 15

Hook: 10 & 12
Tying silk: Black
Tail: Golden pheasant tippets
Rib: Silver wire
Body: Green seal's fur
Hackle: Black
Wing: Mottled feather from grouse's tail

Grouse & Green is a pattern that has historically been more popular than it is today. Some anglers still favour Grouse & Green when the trout are feeding on fry. The pattern has also been tried out as sewin fly and is worth a try as a late evening or post-dawn variant.

Grouse & Purple

PLATE 15

Hook: 10 & 12
Tying silk: Purple
Tail: Golden pheasant tippets
Rib: Silver wire
Body: Purple seal's fur
Hackle: Black
Wing: Mottled feather from grouse's tail

The best of the Grouse series for early season fishing. On small mountain lakes it is used early in April; and, although most of the members of the Grouse series are fancy flies with no claim to suggest any living insect, the Grouse & Purple is used when olives are seen to be hatching.

In mid-Wales the grouse feather has

figured quite prominently in many dressings. Tom Tom of Llangurig made extensive use of the grouse feather and his favourite was: Grugiar ar gorff porffor (Grouse on purple body). The dressing was simple, with only a purple wool body and a small grouse hackle. Three other similar dressings were used on the upper waters of the Wye, Severn, Rheidol and Ystwyth.

Gwybedyn Bach Traed Cochion (Red-legged Gnat)

PLATE 15

Hook: 12 & 14
Tying silk: Black
Rib: Thin gold wire
Body: Thin black silk
Hackle: Coch-a-bon-ddu
Wing: A very light coloured snipe

This is a pattern used in the early season in North Wales and once again the black body is favoured. This brown trout pattern has travelled well and it has proved a firm favourite with many anglers fishing the Teifi Pools. Rainbow trout are not quite so partial to it. The following are two variations of this pattern:

Gwybedyn Bach Du

PLATE 15

Hook: 14
Tying silk: Black
Body: Black silk
Rib: Thin gold wire
Hackle: Black hen
Wing: Starling

The variations are equally effective on lakes and rivers. Some find them more effective than the original.

Gwybedyn Bach Llyn Manod

PLATE 15

Hook: 12
Tying silk: Black
Body: Black silk
Hackle: Black hen
Wing: White duck

Hare's Ear

PLATE 15

Hook: 12 & 14
Tying silk: Yellow
Body: Hare's ear
Hackle: Blue dun

This pattern, designed to fish the River Ogwen and upper waters of the Conway, is tied with yellow silk which shows up prominently through the very sparse fur dressing. The hackle is an important part of the dressing and can have as many as four turns. This hackle, when pulled against the current, produces life in the fly. The pattern possibly represents a nymph in the process of emerging from its shuck and on the point of hatching.

This Welsh tying may not be accepted by the purists on the chalk streams of the south of England but it works on Welsh 'chalkstreams' like the Teifi. On many Welsh rivers, it would probably be taken for the medium spring olive nymph. Darker dun hackles can be used as the season progresses.

The Hare's Ear was used extensively on such rivers as the Usk, Teifi, Severn and the Dee, but more recently it has become very important in its wet form as a nymph on stillwaters. Nymph fishing has given this old pattern a new lease of life and it may become one of the most important flies in

PLATE 9
Alder, Alder (Walker), Red Ant
Black Ant, August Brown, Soldier Beetle
Soldier Beetle (Price), Eric's Beetle, Blackie
Black & Silver, Black Gnat, Black & Peacock Spider

PLATE 10
Black Pennell, Black Quill, Black Spider
Black Spot, Bloody Mary, Bluebottle
Bluebottle (Tannatt), Blue Hen, Blue Ruff
Blue-Winged Olive, Bongoch, Bracken Clock

the stillwater angler's wallet. The original Welsh pattern should be used as the nymph representation of hatching olives.

The Hare's Ear is effective when fished at all levels in stillwaters. Some add lead or copper to the dressing which makes it sink in the water. This is fished with a floating line and a long leader. On Clywedog reservoir in mid-Wales the small Hare's Ear fished in the top layer is very effective.

Hare's Ear Nymph

PLATE 25

Hook: 10 & 12
Tying silk: Yellow
Rib: Gold wire
Body: Hare's ear
Thorax: Peacock herl

Used for many years on Welsh rivers in its traditional form, the Hare's Ear has always been dressed with a light dun hackle and fished downstream. The new approach is to fish it upriver and let it sink deep to move fish that refuse to respond to downstream fishing.

The great advantage of upriver casting is that it allows the nymph to sink deep. The shape of the nymph is ideally designed for quick sinking, especially if it has some lead or copper incorporated into the dressing. The thorax of hare's fur gives the body of the nymph its realistic appearance and the peacock herl represents the wing cases.

Harry Tom

PLATE 15

Hook: 12, 14 & 16
Tying silk: Yellow
Tail: Blue dun fibres
Rib: Gold wire

Body: Dark hare's ear
Hackle: Blue dun
Wing: Bronze mallard

This is an effective stillwater pattern - especially if either pond olives or lake olives are present. A darker dun hackle is required for early season fishing: a lighter honey dun for the summer months.

Harry Tom has proved its value, especially in a good breeze, on predominantly wild brown trout fisheries such as Claerwen, Nantymoch and even as far afield as Loch Leven in Scotland and Lough Conn in County Mayo in Ireland, and it is increasingly used on Welsh rivers where the trout might be taking it for a dark olive dun. It is effective throughout the season on both rivers and stillwaters.

The tendency is to place the Harry Tom on the bob in a three or four-fly cast. This can result in trout slashing at it and not being hooked. Some anglers tie it on small double hooks, which improves the hooking capability of the pattern.

The Harry Tom on the point of the cast can take trout from deeper water and, to this end, it is advisable to add a little lead under the dressing to help it to sink quickly. Fished in this manner it suggests a nymph rising to the surface of the water.

Such is the all-round effectiveness of this fly that it really can be described as a 'fly for all seasons'.

Haul a Gwynt
(Sun and Wind)

PLATE 15

Hook: 12 & 14
Tying silk: Black
Body: Black ostrich herl
Hackle: Small cock pheasant neck feathers
Wing: Black crow

Haul a Gwynt is an easy fly to tie. The ostrich herl makes for a very full body. The correct size of hackle is found some two thirds the way up the cock pheasant's neck. The use of too large a feather results in the black tips not forming a border around the hackle as it should. Many anglers tend to use a bigger pattern in a big wave but it is not always wise to do so. The Haul a Gwynt is effective especially on North Wales stillwaters, on the bob of a wet-fly cast, in a good wave with a stormy breeze.

Haul a Gwynt (variant)

PLATE 15

Hook: 12, 14 & 16
Tying silk: Black
Body: Black chenille or black fur
Hackle: Dark cock pheasant
Wing: Snipe wing
Front hackle: Two turns brown partridge

This is a far heavier version of the Haul a Gwynt which is highly effective on Llyn Trawsfynydd. It generally occupies the bob position - but also seems to work well with a Green Peter on the bob with the Haul a Gwynt fished on the next dropper. This allows it to be fished in the surface film where its bulky hackle creates surface disturbance which excites fish cruising in the vicinity.

Hawthorn Fly

PLATE 15

Hook: 12
Tying silk: Black
Body: Black silk
Thorax: Black wool
Trailing legs: Black nylon (knotted)
Hackle: Black cock

This big black fly makes its appearance in the countryside in May - often when the Hawthorn or May tree is in white blossom. There is no excuse for any angler failing to recognise the fly because its long legs make it look as if its 'under-carriage' were down! It only gets on the water from time to time - blown by the breeze or somehow by accident.

It is effective on rivers and lakes throughout Wales during warm and windy May days, fished either as wet or dry.

Hawthorn Fly (Black Ostrich)

Corff blewyn het ddu a thraed du (Body from black ostrich herl and black legs)

PLATE 15

Hook: 12
Tying silk: Black
Body: Black ostrich herl
Hackle: Black hen

This Welsh pattern makes no reference to its long legs.

Hawthorn Fly (Black Wing)

Adden ddu ar gorff du a choesau du (Black wing on black body with black legs)

PLATE 15

Hook: 12
Tying silk: Black
Body: Black wool or floss
Hackle: Black hen
Wing: Black crow

This pattern comes from the Bethesda area

and is used on local lakes. It is fished in the surface film just as if a hawthorn fly has been caught by the water. The dry fly was not extensively used on the rivers of North Wales - with the exception of the Dee - until the late forties. Prior to that, most anglers practised the wet fly method fished downriver immediately after heavy water. The Hawthorn used mainly in this manner was supposed to represent the adult hawthorn fly blown onto the running water and drowned.

Hen Lambed

PLATE 15

Hook: 10, 12
Tying silk: Yellow
Rib: Flat gold tinsel
Body: Yellow rabbit flax near base of ear
Hackle: Sooty hen
Wing: A thrush wing (now starling or teal) encasing bright yellow dyed goose

This was used as a sedge fly and was a favourite with a number of Ffestioniog fishers. The overall impression achieved by the fly was that of a very light-coloured moth, which fitted it to night fishing.

While it is very important that these old patterns are not lost, it is fair to note that they are not extensively used these days.

Invicta, Black

PLATE 15

Hook: 10
Tying silk: Black
Tail: Golden pheasant toppings
Rib: Silver wire
Body: Black seal's fur
Hackle: Black hen
Wing: Hen pheasant
Front hackle: Blue jay

The Black Invicta is used on the Usk reservoir (*see* Invicta, Silver)

Invicta, Orange

PLATE 16

Hook: 10 Orange tying silk
Tying silk:
Tail: Golden pheasant toppings
Rib: Gold wire
Body: Orange seal's fur
Hackle: Hot orange
Front hackle: Blue jay

Orange Invicta is used on Llandegfedd reservoir. (*see* Invicta, Silver)

Invicta, Silver

PLATE 15

Hook: 10, 12 & 14
Tying silk: Yellow
Tail: Golden pheasant toppings
Rib: Gold wire
Body: Seal's fur dyed yellow
Body hackle: Red cock
Wing: Hen pheasant wing
Front hackle: Blue jay

On many of the big reservoirs of Wales, variations of the Invicta (in at least five different colours) can be seen.

The tail feathers of a hen pheasant do not give a tidy wing, and so feathers from the wing are advised. Many Welsh anglers adopt the Irish tying style, in which they palmer the Invicta with two red cock hackles - thus giving the fly considerable 'kick' when retrieved through the waves.

The Silver Invicta is a handy campaigner - day, evening or night, when all else fails. It is closely related to the Dai Ben.

PLATE 11
Brown Owl, Black Beetle, Butcher
Bloody Butcher, Kingfisher Butcher, Capel Celyn
Chief, Chwilen Ben Glec, Cinnamon Sedge
Cinnamon Sedge (Lane), Cinnamon Sedge (Lunn), Cinnamon Sedge (Tannatt)

Iron Blue Dun

PLATE 16

Hook: 14
Tying silk: Crimson
Tail: Blue dun hackle fibres
Body: Mole fur with crimson showing tail
Hackle: Dark blue dun cock hackle

It is probably true to say that every area in Wales has its own local artificial fly to represent this little chap. It is a favourite with trout and anglers alike. It is an easy fly to identify as it is small - with four wings of dark blue dun. The blue dun (*Baetis pumilus*) varies in size from river to river: it is considerably bigger on the Usk than on the upper Severn or on the Tryweryn, a tributary of the upper Dee.

Iron Blue Dun, Acheson's

PLATE 16

Hook: 9 Kirby
Tying silk: Yellow
Body: Blue fur, with or without yellow silk rib
Hackle: Blue dun hen

Usk flies a hundred and fifty years ago were dressed very lightly and in a manner similar to that practised on the river Clyde in Scotland. The flies that Acheson used were all dressed on a short body, utilising just half the shank, as with low-water salmon fly patterns. This style was unique in Wales as the whole hook shank was always used to support the dressing. During the Rebecca Riots 1839-43, which were the upshot of social unrest in south west Wales, many Welsh estates were victims of heavy poaching as an expression of social revolt. Keepers were therefore brought down from Scotland, and it is thought that some of these keepers may have brought with them the Clyde style of flies which, proving successful on the Usk and other South Wales rivers, were widely copied.

A number of fly patterns on the river Usk have been attributed to a Mr Acheson, on one of the beats.

Acheson adopted the short body to facilitate quick sinking. Trout on the Usk tend to feed high up in the water at certain times. The wet fly should just penetrate the surface on landing; so that it can take the fish just below the surface. Fished in this way, it represents a hatching or a drowned dun. The short body, scant hackle and wings pass for a drowned mature fly.

Iron Blue Dun (Glas Cwta)

PLATE 16

Hook: 14
Tying silk: Claret
Body: Claret quill
Hackle: Almost black with brown tips

On some rivers in the Dee valley the pattern Glas Cwta has been used to imitate the iron blue dun.

Iron Blue Dun, William Roberts'

PLATE 16

Hook: 12 & 14
Tying silk: Claret
Body: Claret wool
Hackle: Dark dun

This pattern is used on the fast flowing rivers of North Wales where it accounts for many a trout whenever the natural is hatching. Other patterns used in various parts of Wales when the iron blue dun is about, include Snipe & Purple, Pheasant Tail, Dark Watchet and Rusty Spinner.

Jack Frost

PLATE 21

Hook: 6, 8 & 10 long shank
Tying silk: Black or white
Body: White Sirdar baby wool covered by one-eighth inch wide strip of polythene
Tail: Crimson wool
Wing: White marabou
Hackle: Long fibres of crimson and white cock hackles

The Jack Frost is a first reserve for the Black Lure with many reservoir anglers. In the cold days of April when the fish are reluctant to move - even to the Black Lure - the first change is invariably to a white lure. The Jack Frost often works. It is a highly visible attractor and, when fished deep in the early season, days of limited light, it does often score over the darker lures.

The Jack Frost is fished deep in cold weather but, as the season progresses, it can be fished up nearer the surface. Used from the boats on Llandegfedd and on Brenig the Jack Frost, stripped back quickly on a floating line, can take cruising fish. It is also very useful later in the season when the big fish are chasing the fry on Llandegfedd and Eglwys Newydd.

Jersey Herd

PLATE 21

Hook: 6, 8 & 10 long shank
Tying silk: Black
Tail and Back: Bronze peacock herl
Body: Under layer - any coloured floss. Over layer - flat copper gold tinsel
Hackle: Hot orange

The Jersey Herd is a lure which should be worked slowly on a slow-sinking line. It can be fished over the shallows. Some anglers fish the Jersey Herd on a long leader with a floating line - as they would a nymph.

There is a tendency for modern flydressers to use gold tinsel for the body instead of the required copper tinsel. It is important that the original dressing is adhered to, as the copper is vastly superior to the gold body. The original material came from milk bottle tops, hence the lure's name.

Ken's Grey Midge

PLATE 25

Hook: 14-16
Tying silk: Grey
Rib: Size 14 oval gold wire
Body: Mole fur
Thorax: Mole fur
Hackle: Blue slate hen
Wing case: Pigeon primary feathers

Ken Bowering is one the most consistent catchers of fish in South Wales. He fishes, in the main, heavily-fished reservoirs, a demanding environment for any fly or nymph pattern. His powers as an international competitive angler are well known, having served in the Welsh team for a number of years and been its captain.

He fishes his Grey Midge on a floating line and keeps the nymph in the surface film. By placing it in the bob position, the nymph is held in the right place for surface-cruising fish.

Kill Devil Spider

PLATE 26

Hook: 14 & 16
Tying silk: Black
Body: Peacock herl

PLATE 12
Cinnamon Sedge (Woolley), Coachman, Hackle Coachman
Lead-Winged Coachman, Royal Coachman, Brecon Cob
Yellow Cob, Orange Cob, Coch-a-bon-ddu
Cochen-las, Coch-yn-las, Cog

PLATE 13
Cogyn Now'r Allt, Concoction, Cord, Egarych Cochddu
Egarych Corff Llygoden Ddwr, Egarych Dyfrgi, Egarych Clust Sgwarnog, Egarych Corff Paun
Cow Dung, Daddy, Crane Fly, Crawshay's Olive
Cream, Dafydd Lloyd, Devonshire Doctor, Diawl Bach
Drudwy Corff Du, Dunkeld, Du'r Fran, Early Brown

Hackle: Long black hen

First devised by David Foster of Ashbourne. The exceptionally long hackle makes for a very attractive fly when it is worked in a fast-flowing current. The long hackle flows back over the plump peacock herl body and gives a very life-like nymph impression.

As these Kill Devil Spiders are dressed on small hooks, it often becomes a major problem to hook the fast-hitting grayling. Some grayling anglers on the river Dee dress the body to cover only the front portion of the hook - in the low-water salmon fly style.

Large Whirling Dun

PLATE 16

Hook: 12
Tying silk: Yellow
Body: Blue squirrel fur and yellow marten mixed, varied occasionally with orange mohair
Hackle: Brown partridge
Wing: Starling

A traditional pattern from the river Usk. Effective early season generally placed in the middle spot of a three-fly cast. A firm favourite with Usk anglers fishing above the town of Brecon.

Light Blue, Usk

PLATE 16

Hook: 12 & 14
Tying silk: Yellow
Body: Yellow wool
Hackle: Pale blue Andalusian hen
Wing: Starling wing

Another good early season pattern tied by Leslie Peters of Brecon. Such is Leslie's reputation that the initials 'L.P' are appended to his variant patterns sold in tackle shops in Brecon. The 'LPLB' pattern is designed to attract trout feeding on the numerous olives that hatch in the early days of the season on the river Usk. The Light Blue flies are in greatest demand around Easter.

Little Chap

PLATE 16

Hook: 16
Tying silk: Crimson
Body: One strand of peacock herl dyed magenta
Hackle: Hen with blue centre and ginger points, or dark blue hen with red points

This fly is extensively used on the rivers of North Wales- -especially on the Ceiriog - in the early part of the season. It is also used on the upper Severn when the February red is about. Often, in the early part of the season, the trout are very difficult to tempt when temperatures are low, but the Little Chap can often rouse them from their torpor.

The pattern was apparently given to G.E.M. Skues by a Wels-man.

Llew Bach (Little Lion)

PLATE 16

Hook: 13 Sneck bend
Tying silk: Black
Rib: Thin gold thread or wire
Body: Black silk
Hackle: Coch-a-bon-ddu or yellow and black based feather
Wing: Dark bronze mallard

A very useful early season fly. It is fished on the lakes and rivers of North Wales in all weather and all water levels, as point or centre fly on a three-fly cast.

There is a bigger version of the Llew Bach, which naturally is known as Y Llew Mawr (The Big Lion). It is the identical dressing on a much bigger hook. The Llew Mawr is used when the river water is coloured or on the lake when the wind is quite strong and the surface of the water ruffled.

Longhorn

PLATE 25

Hook: 10 & 12
Tying silk: Brown
Rib: Gold wire over abdomen
Body: Abdomen - blue, green or amber
Thorax: Chestnut or sepia
Hackle: Brown partridge
Horns: Two pheasant tail fibres tied long

Welsh anglers have always looked forward to the sedge fishing time when they would arrive on the river at nightfall and fish their Sedge patterns on the surface.

The Sedge Pupa has become increasingly popular at this time of day with patterns like the Longhorn doing well. The Longhorn fished in the sink-and-draw method on a floating line represents the sedge pupa coming up in the water.

The Longhorns (*Athripsodes cinereus*), especially the green version, have done well on Clywedog, Brenig and the Teifi Pools.

Macrel Bach

PLATE 16

Hook: 12 & 14
Tying silk: Purple
Body: Purple floss
Hackle: Black hen
Wing: Bronze mallard

This is a pattern for the rivers of North Wales where it is considered an early season fly. It bears a close resemblance to the Snipe & Purple and the Usk Purple and, no doubt, is at its most effective when the iron blue dun is hatching. Many fishermen love to have the odd colourful fly like this in their wallets. It is fished downstream as a wet fly.

Mallard & Claret

PLATE 16

Hook: 10, 12 & 14
Tying silk: Claret
Tail: Golden pheasant tippets
Rib: Gold wire
Body: Claret seal's fur
Hackle: Ginger or claret
Wing: Bronze mallard

This is the standard tying of the Mallard & Claret which is probably one of the best-known wet flies in use today. It is used on most Welsh lakes and reservoirs and to a lesser extent on Welsh rivers. In Wales, however, there are a host of variations.

Aden ceiliog hwyaden ar gorff paun a thraed cochion.
(A mallard wing on a peacock body and ginger legs).

Hook: 12
Tying silk: Brown
Body: Peacock herl
Hackle: Ginger
Wing: Mallard

This pattern is not a copy of any known natural insect. As a point fly it is generally used in the lower layers of the water and the technique is to cast the fly out and give ample time for it to sink and bring it back with the traditional figure-of-eight retrieve.

Aden ceiliog hwyaden ar gorff lliw gwin a thraed du-flaengoch.
(A bronze mallard wing on wine coloured body with coch-a-bon-ddu legs).

Hooks: 12
Tying silk: Black
Body: Claret wool
Hackle: Coch-a-bon-ddu
Wing: Bronze mallard

This is the Welsh forerunner of the modern Mallard & Claret minus a tail.

Aden ceiliog hwyaden ar gorff lliw cochddu a thraed duon.
(Bronze mallard wing on black/red body with black legs).

Hook: 12
Tying silk: Black
Body: Red/Black wool
Hackle: Black
Wing: Bronze mallard

This variation of the Mallard series is favoured in August and September. It is always used as a point fly and is retrieved slowly. In some of the old flies examined, the wing was tied very short and would look very much like a wing case when pulled quickly through the water. A number of present-day anglers favour this pattern above the popular Mallard & Claret on sale in tackle shops.

Aden ceiliog hwyaden ar gorff coch tywyll a thraed cochion.
(Bronze mallard wing on a dark red body with ginger legs).

Hook: 12
Tying silk: Brown
Body: Dark red wool
Hackle: Ginger
Wing: Bronze mallard

This is the least known and used of the Mallard series but it has found favour with most anglers in the Dee valley and on the river Ceiriog.

Aden ceiliog hwyaden ar gorff osidan du main a thraed duon.
(A bronze mallard wing on thin black body with black legs).
Hook: 12
Tying silk: Black
Body: Black silk
Hackle: Black hen
Wing: Bronze mallard

Another black fly with a mallard wing. Invariably used on the point and fished low in the water.

March Brown

PLATE 16

Hook: 12
Tying silk: Copper-coloured
Tail: Two strands from partridge tail
Rib: Yellow thick silk
Body: Hare's ear and yellow hair mixed
Hackle: Brown partridge
Wing: Inner quill feather of pheasant wing

The March Brown is one of the most essential flies on the rivers of Wales during the early part of the season. On the rivers Usk and Teifi, the natural March brown (*Rithrogena haarupi*) hatches in great numbers with the accompaniment of tremendous excitement among the trout. The natural insect has two setae, mottled brown wings and a brownish body. The abundant nymphs are more important food items on Welsh rivers than either the dun or the spinner stage. In this nymph form the March brown is easily available to trout and wet fly patterns are most effective.

It is fished as middle fly on a three-fly cast, down river.

George Scotcher, in his superb little volume, *A Fly Fisher's Legacy*, gives a vivid account of this most important fly for Welsh waters that can hardly be improved on 176 or so years later. He says:

'If, during this season you are early at the river, you must first throw the four-winged brown, then the blue dun, and just before you expect the March brown to come on, throw that, and continue till two o'clock, and then return to the blue dun'.

See also March Brown (Dai Lewis), the dry version.

March Brown, Edmonds'

PLATE 16

Hook: 12
Tying silk: Orange
Body: Orange silk dubbed with rabbit fur (from neck) lightly tinged with red
Hackle: Mottled brown feather from snipe's rump

Edmonds' pattern has its followers but, other than on a few tributaries of the Severn and the Wye, it is not so commonly used as the standard March Brown.

March Brown Nymph

PLATE 25

Hook: 12
Tying silk: Claret
Tail: Honey dun whisks
Rib: Gold wire
Body: Claret seal's fur
Legs: Dark honey dun
Wing case: Pheasant tail herl tied over

Rithrogena haarupi is one of the better known nymphs, common on many rivers in most parts of Wales.

This nymph of the March brown is a stone-clinger and it favours rivers with a stone and gravelly bottom. The nymphs appear in mid-April in great numbers and there is little doubt that the trout often take the nymph in preference to the dun: hence the importance of the nymph to the angler. During low flows the up-stream nymph is preferred to the down-river-and-across method.

March Brown Nymph Variant

PLATE 25

Hook: 12
Tying silk: Yellow
Tail: Two strands of pheasant tail
Body: Orange silk ribbed with gold wire
Thorax: Yellow seal's fur
Wing case: Over seal's fur
Legs: Partridge hackle

March Brown Quill

PLATE 16

Hook: 13
Tying silk: Brown
Body: Peacock quill
Hackle: Brown partridge
Wing: Hen pheasant wing (optional)

Quill bodies have lost a lot of their appeal for tyers in the last 25 years. This is probably the result of flydressers not being prepared to take the same trouble as the fly tyers of old did with their patterns. The March Brown Quill was a fly that served well when the water was clear, in normal and low river flow. It deserves to be better remembered.

The normal season for the March Brown is early Spring and the tendency is for other summer patterns to be more productive thereafter. Yet it is not always advisable to be in too much of a hurry to discard the March Brown as it tends to remain effective long after the natural has disappeared. This is particularly true of the March Brown Quill. It should be fished wet fly downstream; but when the river is low it should be fished upstream.

March Brown, Dai Evans' Usk

PLATE 16

Hook: 12-14
Tying silk: Brown
Tail: White gallina dyed dark sepia
Body & Hackle: Dubbed mixture of black rabbit fur, seal's fur in black and claret and a little fiery brown fur
Wing case: Dark turkey feather

This somewhat complex pattern is known on the Usk but does not have much to recommend it when far simpler versions of the March Brown are used successfully on the river. This is a possible fly to try if the angler sees some inadequacy in the conventional March Brown patterns.

Marlow Buzz

PLATE 16

Hook: 12
Tying silk: Black
Rib: Flat gold
Body: Bronze peacock herl
Hackle: Furnace

This is a close relation of the Coch-a-bon-ddu. The only difference in the dressing is the ribbing of the body with gold flat tinsel and the use of furnace hackle instead of the coch-a-bon-ddu. It is open to question

whether the trout can discern one pattern from another. As with the Coch-a-bon-ddu the Marlow Buzz is best fished as a dropper - and, on the highland lakes, it is most productive in late June and July.

Representing *Phyllopertha horticola*, it is fished in the lakes and rivers of South Wales in the warm weather of June and July.

Missionary

PLATE 21

Hook: 6, 8 & 10 long shank
Tying silk: Black
Tail: Scarlet dyed hackle
Rib: Silver tinsel
Body: White chenille
Wing: Whole silver mallard breast feather
Hackle: Scarlet-dyed cock feathers

The Missionary, like many other white-bodied lures, imitates the fry on which the larger fish feed - especially towards the end of the season. Most anglers cast it out on a lead-core line and wait for it to sink. As the line nears the bottom, the lure is pulled under the water. This action is known as the 'drop'.

The Missionary is especially suitable for the 'drop' in that the whole wing tends to open and this slow, fluttering action is very attractive to fish.

The Missionary can also be used in sewin fishing in the same way. Both in lakes and in the river when fishing the drop. It often pays the angler to have one continuous pull when retrieving - as opposed to the short, jerking motion or the figure-of-eight retrieve. But if being fished on floating line to imitate injured fry, it *should* be fished jerkily.

Muddler Minnow

PLATE 21

Hook: 6, 8 & 10 long shank; 6, 8 & 10 normal shank
Tying silk: Black
Tail: Small section of turkey tail
Body: Flat gold tinsel
Inner wing: Bunch of grey squirrel
Outer wing: Two sections of mottled black turkey wing feather
Head: Natural deer hair

The Muddler Minnow, a North American salmon and trout lure has, in a very short time, proved to be one of the most versatile of game fishing lures. It is a favourite with all boat anglers. It is effective when fished either on the point or on the bob. It produces a very lively effect when used with a sinking line because the deer hair head makes it extremely buoyant: thus it always tends towards an upward movement in the water. When used with a very fast sinking line the Muddler keeps clear of the bottom, thus avoiding snags.

Initially a large lure, the Muddler Minnow is now also used in much smaller sizes (size eight or smaller) especially by boat anglers.

Sewin anglers find the Muddler Minnow very useful at dusk. Then it is used on a floating or a slow sinking line, fished in the upper layers of the water like a surface lure to resemble a struggling moth.

As with all successful patterns, the Muddler Minnow has many variations, the two most successful being the Black Muddler and the White Muddler (see following dressings).

Muddler, Black

PLATE 22

Hook: 6, 8 & 10

Tying silk: Black
Body: Black floss body
Wing: Black squirrel tail
Head: Natural deer hair

Muddler, White

PLATE 22

Hook: 6, 8 & 10 long shank
Tying silk: White
Body: White fluorescent wool
Wing: White marabou
Head: Natural deer hair

Nailer, Dai's

PLATE 17

Hook: 13
Tying silk: Green
Rib: Gold wire
Body: Green silk
Hackle: Blue dun

This is another wet fly from the stable of Dai Lewis. It has a reputation as a rough-weather fly.

Not often used today, it is designed for early season windy weather and low water flows, on the River Teifi.

Nailer, Usk

PLATE 17

Hook: 12 & 14
Tying silk: Purple
Tail: Blue dun
Rib: Gold wire
Body: Five strands of well-marked bronze mallard
Hackle: Blue dun

The Usk Nailer is used on the river Usk when the early olives are about. This is a pattern of considerable merit - with grand conquests to its credit on the upper Usk and its tributaries.

It was first devised to fish the river Usk on a three-fly cast. The practice was to cast it downriver and let it swing round with the current. In recent years, more anglers have been fishing this wet fly pattern upriver. The Usk Nailer works well with this approach.

The body of bronze mallard is an attractive colour and represents the nymph of the olive family. A darker dun feather works better as the season advances. Some dressers like to show some of the purple silk at the tail-end of the fly.

Increasingly popular for lake and reservoir fishing and it is really worth a try when the buzzers are hatching in late evening.

Oak Fly

PLATE 17

Hook: 12 & 13
Tying silk: Orange
Body: Hot orange floss ribbed with grey ostrich herl
Wings: Woodcock secondary quill
Hackle: Furnace cock hackle

There is some doubt as to whether this fly is really as important as it was formerly believed to be. Pryce Tannatt produced an excellent pattern and there is no doubt that the artificial can be effective on its day. Another name for the fly is the Down-looker, because of the tendency of the natural fly (*Leptis scolopacea*) to rest its head downwards.

Scotcher did not tie an artificial but caught the naturals and dapped them.

It is fished early season on the rivers of mid-Wales.

Old Joe

PLATE 17

Hook: 13
Tying silk: Black
Tail: Three strands of pheasant tail
Rib: Silver wire
Body: Pheasant tail herl
Hackle: Olive

This is an early-season fly used on the rivers of mid and north Wales. There is no doubt that it can rival the better-known Pheasant Tail as a point fly. It is at its best when the iron blues are about.

Some of the early dressers of Old Joe insisted that the quality of the body material was important. Cock pheasant tail fibres come in different shades and varying quality. The best shade is that of a deep rich rust with a coppery tinge, and a metallic sheen overall. Old Joe is used in dry or wet form - depending on the condition of the water. During low river levels the dry fly scores well while the wet fly is far superior in times of high water flows. It is a point fly and is usually fished downriver.

Old Warrier

PLATE 17

Hook: 12
Tying silk: Black
Body: Peacock quill
Hackle: Light blue dun

The Old Warrior is a firm favourite with anglers of the Glyn-Neath area and, as with most of the flies devised by Ernest Lewis, they are often as effective on other rivers as they are on the Neath where they were first developed.

The Old Warrior, although similar to the normal Blue Upright pattern, differs in that the hackle is of a considerably lighter hue.

Fish it mid-day early season, in low or mid-water as a normal wet fly downstream, or as an up-river point fly.

Orl

PLATE 17

Hook: 12, 14
Tying silk: Red
Body: Peacock herl
Rib: Red tying silk
Hackle: Blue dun

This pattern came to the Upper Teifi Valley by courtesy of Dan Jones. It has gained its place on the Teifi, many anglers using it instead of the Alder. It is also popular on the stillwater lakes of mid-Wales which have stocks of wild brown trout. The Orl tied on the middle dropper of a three-fly cast is the normal practice.

It is an excellent fly on Talybont reservoir, near Brecon. This fly should not be confused with the Alder - an error made by Courtney Williams.

Palmer, Black

PLATE 17

Hook: 10-14
Tying silk: Black
Rib: Silver wire
Body: Black wool
Hackle: Two black cocks

There are numerous lakes in the Harlech area, and on some of these the Black Palmer is used in May and June. It works well, especially if the hawthorn is about.

Palmer, Badger or Grizzly

PLATE 17

Hook: 14 & 16
Tying silk: Black
Rib: Silver wire
Tag (optional): Red wool
Body: Black silk
Hackle: Grizzle cocks tied palmer

The Badger Palmer is a favourite on the small mountain streams in high summer. It is also used increasingly as a sewin fly. Often, on nights when there is a lot of moonlight, a Badger Palmer fished up-river - as one would fish a dry fly - can do quite well.

The custom with dilettante dressers is to add a little tag or other bits and pieces to a pattern in an attempt, no doubt, to improve it. Recently dressed Badger Palmers have sprouted red tags, but this has not especially helped the fly in its role of fishing for sewin at night. Sewin are notorious bottom pinchers, especially so on a moonlit night! Anything that assists this behaviour is a real disadvantage: although it has to be said that it is as often the head of the fly that is the object of their attentions as much as the posterior end.

The Grizzly Palmer (as it is locally known) is quite a favourite with anglers in the Corwen area on the river Dee. It is used for fishing the excellent grayling that are there. Mike Green, a dresser of exceptional ability, ties them on sizes 14 & 16 with the short, red tag.

Palmer, Red

PLATE 17

Hook: 10-14
Tying silk: Red

Rib: Gold wire
Body: Red wool or seal's fur
Hackle: Two red cock hackles tied palmer fashion

In mid-Wales, the Red Palmer has always been the most popular version of Palmer series.

Palmered flies are easy to tie but it is advisable to get two hackles of different sizes and to use the smaller one to take the hackle down along the body. The shorter fibre, when palmered down along the body, not only makes the fly more pleasing aesthetically but it also facilitates hooking.

Palmered flies are often used as bob flies. The angler casts out some fifteen yards and brings the flies back, with the bob fly just skipping the surface of the water. The trout often splash at a palmered fly fished thus: so the angler will find it advantageous to fish the bob fly in the surface layer and, by lifting the rod, pull the bob fly up and on to the surface.

The Red Palmer can be fished wet or dry fly all summer, on rivers and lakes.

Parry's Black Spider

PLATE 17

Hook: 13
Tying silk: Black
Tag: Silver
Body: Black quill
Hackle: Starling

Black flies have always been popular in Wales and Parry's Black Spider is among the best of them. It is advisable to rib all quill bodies with thin wire to protect the quill from being damaged by the trout's teeth. The latest device to protect quill bodies is to coat them with a thin layer of Super Glue. This binds the whole body into a solid unit and treated flies can survive the capture of some three dozen trout!

The hackle is generally taken from a black hen - but for anglers who use it in rough water or as a bob fly, then a short cock hackle is to be preferred. Parry's Black Spider should be fished downstream, in a three-fly cast.

Partridge & Black

PLATE 17

Hook: 13 & 14
Body: Black silk
Hackle: Well marked partridge

The partridge feather was the most important feather of all for fly dressers in Wales at the turn of the century. On small rivers, the Partridge & Black can still be effective, as a late-season fly, as a dropper.

This pattern represents, loosely, the black gnat (*Bibio johannis*). It is best fished on the rivers of North Wales. There are many Partridge variations. Two are as follows:

Partridge Buzzer (*Pluen petrisen ar gorff cochddu*)

(Partridge hackle on red/black body).

This fly is for the lakes of Wales from June onwards. It is dressed very sparsely, in keeping with the practice of fishing the pattern towards dusk when it is probably taken as a buzzer. Black cotton provides a rib to represent the segmented body.

Partridge & Hare (*Pluen petrisen ar flewyn glust ysgyfarnog*)

(Partridge hackle on a hare's ear body).

This stone fly imitation is fished on the first dropper and dances on and in the surface the river. Usually fished downstream, this pattern also does well for the up-river approach, if the water is extremely low.

Peter Ross

PLATE 17

Hook: 6, 8 & 10 for sewin; 10, 12 & 14 for trout
Tying silk: Black
Tail: Golden pheasant tippets
Rib: Silver wire
Body: Rear half silver, front half dubbing of red seal's fur
Hackle: Black hen
Wing: Teal flank or breast feather

Peter Ross, a shopkeeper from Killin in Perthshire, is reputed to have said of his newly-created fly that he cared little what the trout took it for as long as they liked it. There existed a school of thought that it was taken by the trout for a shrimp, but others believe that it is a fair representation of a small fish. It differs only slightly from the much older and trusted pattern the Teal & Red.

Sewin anglers have great faith in this pattern. On rivers like the Ystwyth and the Rheidol it will take sewin when the river is running high during daylight hours. It also performs well during the hours of darkness and, as is the current fashion, it is being dressed in great tandem lengths and on bigger irons.

Pheasant Tail

PLATE 17

Hook: 14
Tying silk: Crimson
Tail: Three long herls from saddle hackle
Rib: Four turns of gold twist
Body: A very dark herl of cock pheasant tail

feather
Hackle: Honey dun

The pattern favoured by G.E.M. Skues possesses the attractive quality of the ruddy herl of cock pheasant tail. This pattern (dressing above), by Payne Collier uses the dark herl from a cock pheasant tail. This dark version has found more favour with anglers in Wales. On the Teifi and upper Wye, where the pattern is highly regarded, the hackle used is generally of a dark dun, some anglers even favouring a black hackle.

This is an excellent point fly for the normal three-wet-fly cast fished in the traditional downstream manner early in the season. Many anglers swear that the Pheasant Tail is at its best when the iron blues are about.

Pheasant Tail Nymph

PLATE 26

Hook: 10 & 12
Tying silk: Hot orange
Rib: Gold wire
Tail & body: Rusty pheasant tail fibres
Thorax: Hare's ear fur

On the rivers Usk and Teifi, presentation of the nymph up-river often brings success on the cold, early days of the season. The fish are then low in the water and the normal wet fly does not get down to them. Some anglers add a layer of lead under the dressing of the Pheasant Tail in order to help it to sink quickly.

The Pheasant Tail used on stillwaters is generally on a bigger hook and is fished on a long leader with a floating line.

Pluen 'Rhen Law
(Old Boy's Fly)

PLATE 17

Hook: 12-14, wide gape
Tying silk: Purple
Tail: Two strands of horse hair
Body: Reddish purple wool
Hackle: Black
Wing: Hen pheasant tail with a sliver of light dun on either side.

Another local pattern which has travelled well and earned its place on the casts of lake fishers in areas other than its native Ffestiniog. It is sometimes mistakenly called a 'Haul a Gwynt' because it is effective when conditions are sunny and windy. As many Ffestiniog anglers in the past were quarrymen, in full-time employment from dawn to dusk, it is only natural that the Ffestiniog flies earned a reputation for catching well at night.

As to the identity of 'yr hen law' - the old hand or old expert who created the fly - we shall never know. Lost in the mists of Snowdonia.

Poacher

PLATE 17

Hook: 10, 12 & 14
Tying silk: Brown
Tag: Red wool
Body: Rear portion, yellow seal's fur; front portion, peacock herl
Hackle: Coch-a-bon-ddu hen or cock

This bob pattern came from Loch Lomond but has been adopted in Wales as an alternative to the Coch-a-bon-ddu. In recent years it has proved particularly effective on rainbow trout fisheries.

Pupil Teacher

PLATE 17

Hook: 12
Tying silk: Black
Rib: Gold wire
Body: Peacock herl
Hackle: Blue dun hackle

This fly has been a great favourite in South Wales especially on the small rivers which were tributaries of the bigger and often polluted rivers. Dan Jones of Ferndale, Dan the Fisherman, says that more fish were taken on the 'PT' than on any other fly in the coal mining area of the South.

It is used as a bob fly.

Rhwyfwr Tinwyrdd
(Green-tailed Sedge)

PLATE 14

Hook: 12
Tying silk: Brown
Tag: Gold wire
Body: Wool from black sheep, with green blob on bend of hook
Wing: Brown owl with partridge tail wing between the matched wing.

This is without doubt the most important trout fly for the majority of river fishers in Wales. It is often compared with the Mayfly and there are many similarities. The pattern used in North Wales was known as Rhwyfwr Tinwyrdd.

Roger Woolley

PLATE 18

Hook: 10 & 12
Tying silk: Claret
Rib: Gold wire
Body: Claret fur

Hackle: Dark green
Wing: Bronze mallard

Roger Woolley was one of the great professional flydressers of the 1930s. This pattern, which makes early use of the dyed hackle, has been successful on the Ffestiniog lakes of North Wales.

Sedge, Big (or Big Boatman) Rhwyfwyr Mawr Cochddu

PLATE 18

Hook: 8
Tying silk: Black
Body: Originally Wool from the scrotum of a black ram. A modern alternative is a mixture of dark brown and claret wool
Rib: Gold thin wire
Wing: Brown owl encasing partridge tail
Hackle: Brown partridge

This was considered to be the most important sedge fly in North Wales. It was dressed bulkily and represented the big mouthful that trout expect in the late evening when the great red sedge is about.

The sedge group of flies is a very large group - representing nearly 200 different species. They are, in the main, nocturnal - with a few of the smaller ones hatching out in the afternoons. This can be used as a highly buoyant bob fly, or as a dry pattern. It is devised with two pairs of wings (as in the adult sedge fly). The hackle is put on rather liberally so that the overall effect is of a big bushy insect.

Sedge, Green-Ringed Rhwyfwyr Clychau Gwyrdd

PLATE 18

Hook: 10

Tying silk: Green
Body: Wool from scrotum of a black ram or dark brown/claret wool
Rib: Green silk
Hackle: Brown partridge
Wing: Light coloured brown owl (subst.)

In recent years the brook trout has been introduced into many fisheries in Wales - not always with great success - and this cheerful pattern, fished on the bob, has proved effective for taking this new breed of trout. The fly is at its best when brought speedily back along the surface of the water, causing a wake.

Sedge, Small Rhwyfwyr Cochddu Bach

PLATE 18

Hook: 12
Tying silk: Black
Body: Wool from the scrotum of a black ram, or dark brown/claret
Rib: Thin gold wire
Wing: Brown owl (substitute) encasing partridge tail
Hackle: Brown partridge

Anglers on the lakes of Blaenau Ffestiniog use the smaller version of the Big Sedge in the early part of the evening. Used when the little brown sedge and the little red sedge are in evidence.

Sedge, Teal-Wing Rhwyfwyr Cochddu Aden Telsan

PLATE 18

Hook: 10 & 12
Tying silk: Black
Body: Wool from scrotum of a black ram, or dark brown/claret wool

Rib: Thin gold wire
Hackle: Brown partridge
Wing: Teal flank feathers

A late-season performer and fished best in August. The teal wing is of the off-white variety and not the well-marked one. This fly took an impressive basket of fish when fished as a bob fly from a boat on Llysyfran Reservoir.

Sedge, Teifi Pools

PLATE 19

Hook: 10 & 12
Tying silk: Brown
Body: Orange wool or orange seal's fur
Hackle: Dark ginger
Wing: Light dun

Dr Roderick who discovered this fly enjoyed fishing the Teifi Pools, and his favourite ploy was to fish the far bank of Llyn Teifi by letting his flies skim along the surface. The wild brown trout responded well to this. It is a pattern worth carrying in the fly box, though Dr Roderick's faith in it is not always borne out. The secret seems to lie in the movement of the fly, quickly, on a floating line along the surface when used as a bob fly. In my opinion, it works better during the summer months and towards evening after a particularly hot bright day.

Shrimp (E. H. Turner)

Hook: 11 shrimp hook
Tying silk: Brown
Body: Underlayer of copper wire. Pale brown wool - tied to form a hump
Hackle: Red cock palmered
Back: Golden pheasant tippet fibres pulled right over body to form a wing case and tied in at head

This pattern was created by Eric Horsfall

Turner for use on the river Derwent. Eric's creations, because of his association with mid-Wales, were soon tried out on Welsh rivers. The Shrimp pattern found little support when it was fished in the normal wet-fly method. Things improved dramatically, however, when it was fished directly down-river and worked with movement of the rod. Long rods are an asset to this type of fishing.

Smokey Blue

PLATE 18

Hook: 13 & 14
Tying silk: Yellow
Body: Mole fur
Hackle: Covert feather from water hen's wing

Pryce Tannatt used this wet pattern to represent the iron blue dun and the dark olive. The dressing was applied very sparsely with a small amount of mole fur being used and the yellow silk showing through the dressing.

The Smokey Blue is a capital wet fly in the early days of the season.

The upper Severn holds a good stock of grayling. The Smokey Blue is known to have done well with these fish on size 16 hooks.

Soldier Beetle (Pryce Tannatt)

PLATE 9

Hook: 10 & 12
Tying silk: Hot orange
Body: Golden pheasant tippets tied in, having a dark bar at the extreme end, carried over and fastened at shoulder. The body of hot orange floss.
Hackle: Bright ginger cock

Pryce Tannatt, during his time in Wales, must have seen thousands of these insects (*Cantharis rustica*) in late summer. His pattern bears a close relationship to those given by Taff Price and Eric Horsfall Turner, both of whom have or had connections in mid-Wales.

Soldier Beetle (Taff Price)

PLATE 9

Hook: 12
Tying silk: Hot orange
Body: Orange floss
Wing case: Brown raffene, the tail end marked with a black felt pen
Hackle: Natural red

Recently, in a competition on one of the mid-Wales reservoirs, soldier beetles were swarming all over the place and being blown onto the water. The trout were quick to receive the manna - which does not come that often from the heavens of the mountain regions. Taff's pattern proved to be more attractive than either that of Eric Horsfall Turner or Pryce Tannatt. It was taken in both wet and dry form.

Stone Fly

PLATE 18

Hook: 12
Tying silk: Yellow
Body: Dirty yellow wool
Hackle: Brown partridge

There are many rivers in Wales where stone flies (*Perla maxima*) represent the most important section of a trout's diet and it is surprising that, on the whole, little attention has been paid to them. On quick-flowing, rain-fed rivers these flies are found in abundance and any angler who does not carry a few artificial representations in his fly box will one day regret it. The most important members of the stone fly order are February red, early brown, large stone fly and the willow fly. Another member is the yellow sally which has fewer adherents piscine or human - from experience.

Some anglers are on record as saying that the natural is too difficult to copy, and hence to try to do so is a waste of time. On fast-flowing rivers the artificial does not need to be anywhere near so accurately represented as on more gentle-flowing rivers, so all the angler is really looking for is a match in size and general appearance.

Stone Fly, Dark (Alan Hudson)

PLATE 18

Hook: 14-16
Tying silk: Black
Rib: Silver or gold medium tinsel
Body: Hare's ear
Hackle: Badger front and black cock behind

A good pattern for the rivers of North Wales.

Hook: 12 & 10
Tying silk: Brown
Body: Hare's ear ribbed with yellow silk
Wing: Woodcock
Hackle: A well-marked cree with a palmered grizzle

The large stone flies (*Perla carlukiana* and *Perla cephalotes*) are of interest since they are very widely distributed in Wales. A pattern mainly used on the upper Severn, it has, curiously, gained a good reputation on the upper Towy and Taf. The above version of the fly is tied rather bulkily - with the wing extending beyond the bend of the hook.

Stone Fly, Parry's

PLATE 18

Hook: 12
Tying silk: Yellow
Body: Hare's ear
Hackle: A well marked cree and a badger
(two turns only)

An imitation of the February red, this is by far the most important of the stone flies on rivers Teifi, Severn, Dee and Taf.

Stone Fly (Scotcher)

PLATE 18

Hook: 12-14
Tying silk: Black
Hackle: Dark freckled cock
Body: Black and yellow sheep's wool ribbed with waxed yellow silk
Wing (optional): Mallard wing

A very old dressing from Scotcher's classic book *The Flyfishers Legacy*.

Sweeny Todd
(Richard Walker)

PLATE 22

Hook: 6, 8 & 10 Long shank
Tying silk: Black
Body: Black floss with a collar of neon magenta fluorescent wool at root of wing
Wing: Black squirrel

This is one of the best lures for rainbow trout. It is used in the early days of the season and the spot of magenta wool often triggers off the attack.

It seems that this comparatively modern pattern had a fore-runner at the end of the last century in Wales, known as the Bongoch. This old pattern had a red spot at the base of the wing and many of the quarrymen of Blaenau Ffestiniog were happy to use it in the month of August - especially in a big wind.

The Sweeny Todd can be used in very small sizes on the rivers of Wales in the early days of the season. Many patterns devised for the productive reservoirs in England have not registered the same degree of success when used on Welsh reservoirs. The Sweeny Todd is the exception.

Teal & Black

PLATE 18

Hook: 8, 10 & 12
Tying silk: Black
Tail: Golden pheasant tippets
Rib: Silver wire
Body: Black seal's fur
Hackle: Black hen
Wing: From teal breast or flank

In the early part of this century the Teal & Black in size eight was considered to be the all-important point fly to fish for sewin at night. Its ribbed black body and barred wing make for a very good colour pattern - hence a very attractive fly.

Teal, Blue & Silver

PLATE 18

Hook: 6, 8, 10 & 12 Tandem and tube style
Tying silk: Black
Tail: Golden pheasant tippets
Rib: Silver wire
Body: Flat wire
Hackle: Bright blue
Wing: Teal breast or flank feathers

This fly is, without doubt, the fore-runner of all modern sewin flies. Its variants are numerous and collectively take something like fifty per cent of all the sewin taken on a fly in Wales. The standard dressing gives teal feather for the wing but hair wings are increasingly popular. Hair wings are far more responsive to water currents, and offer vastly more interesting colour ranges than do the more solid fibre wings.

In its tandem form, the Teal, Blue & Silver is designed to be used with a quick-sinking line and to work in the deep section of the pool. Here the big sewin tend to stay, and the deep-sunk Teal, Blue & Silver often tempts them.

While the pattern is considered to be mainly a river pattern, it finds itself being increasingly used on some reservoirs - and anglers using it have taken impressive bags of rainbow trout from places like Clywedog and Elan Valley.

Teal & Green

PLATE 18

Hook: 8, 10 & 12
Tying silk: Black
Tail: Golden pheasant tippets
Rib: Silver wire
Body: Green seal's fur
Hackle: Black hen or cock
Wing: Teal flank or breast feather

More of a lake fly than a river fly. Dressed on a number twelve hook, it is effective as a member of a wet-fly team fished on a slow sinking line on stillwaters. Some anglers like to use it in rough conditions, whilst others feel it is a very good fly to use when the trout are after the minnows.

Teal & Mixed

PLATE 19

Hook: 8 & 10
Tying silk: Black

Tail: Golden pheasant tippets
Rib: Silver wire
Body: One-third each of yellow, red and blue dubbing of seal's fur
Hackle: Black hen or cock
Wing: Teal flank or breast feathers

The most colourful of the teal family but not so widely used as the other members. It is a pattern that has its devotees and, in the days before the Brianne Dam was built on the upper waters of the river Towy, the Teal & Mixed covered considerable mileage there in those beautiful and desolate mountain rapids towards the tail end of the season.

Teal & Red

PLATE 18

Hook: 8 & 10
Tying silk: Black
Tail: Golden pheasant tippets
Rib: Silver wire
Body: Red seal's fur
Hackle: Black hen or cock
Wing: Teal flank or breast feathers

This fly could well have been the forerunner of the Peter Ross pattern. It can do well on the sewin rivers of mid-Wales - especially in water which is slightly coloured.

Troellwr Corff Llygoden Ddwr (Nightjar & Rat)

PLATE 19

Hook: 12
Tying silk: Yellow
Body: Water rat fur
Hackle: Black hen
Wing: Originally nightjar, now grouse

This pattern, as with indeed most of the Nightjar series, is not well known outside the Ffestiniog area. The fact that nightjars are now strictly protected and no longer common birds is the reason for this! Nevertheless this pattern can be used with substitute feathers from the grouse. It is a daytime pattern, especially effective early in the season.

The Alaw reservoir in Anglesey was at one time renowned for its big brown trout. Some anglers even used to come over from Ireland to fish for them. Troellwr flies were the ones that took these trout in the early days of the season. They were also effective on the Brenig reservoir with the native brown trout that are found there. Some flies work better with brown trout than they do with rainbows: this is certainly true of the Troellwr Corff Llygoden Ddwr.

Troellwr Mawr
(Big Nightjar) Dafydd Dafis

PLATE 19

Hook: 10
Tying silk: Claret
Body: Reddish purple seal's fur ribbed with golden thread
Hackle: Black hen
Wing: Originally nightjar, now grouse

This 'wet weather fly' has been used extensively in the stony sections of the North Wales lakes where it has taken fish that were down deep.

Troellwr Mawr
(Big Nightjar) John Owen

PLATE 19

Hook: 10
Tying silk: Red
Body: Red seal's fur ribbed with gold wire
Hackle: Dark coch-a-bon-ddu

Wing: Originally nightjar, now grouse

This pattern, created by John Owen, differs only slightly from the previous one dressed by Dafydd Dafis. This is one of those patterns that, like the recipes of the ancient Physicians of Myddfai, were highly confidential family trade secrets.

Snipe & Purple

PLATE 19

Hook: 14
Tying silk: Purple
Body: Purple floss
Hackle: Snipe hackle

The Snipe & Purple pattern is better known in other parts of the United Kingdom, and both the Usk purple and the Macrel Bach are considered better patterns for fast-flowing rivers. The tendency is for the snipe hackle to wrap itself around the purple body, while in the other two patterns the hackle 'kicks' and imbues a little life into the fly. Some anglers of late have been using a well marked cree hackle instead of snipe for the Snipe & Purple.

Snipe & Yellow

PLATE 19

Hook: 14
Tying silk: Yellow
Body: Yellow floss
Hackle: Snipe hackle

The Snipe & Yellow is taken by the trout for a variety of insects including the nymphs of the olive and of the stone flies.

Usk Dark Blue

PLATE 19

Hook: 12 & 14
Tying silk: Black
Body: Mole fur
Hackle: Dark blue hen, nearly black if possible
Wing: Moorhen

The Usk Dark Blue takes trout feeding on the early and dark olives that hatch in March and April.

Usk Purple

PLATE 19

Hook: 12 & 14
Tying silk: Purple
Body: Purple floss
Hackle: Dark blue dun
Wing: Snipe wing (blue dun)

This old Usk pattern, an early season favourite, is taken for the iron blue nymph. It is closely related to the Snipe & Purple and has the reputation of fishing better on cold days. The Usk Purple is generally fished in the middle of a three-fly cast.

This pattern is similar to one in common use in the Snowdon area of North Wales, known as Macrel Bach.

Water Cricket

PLATE 19

Hook: 13 & 14
Tying silk: Purple
Body: Hot orange silk floss ribbed with tying silk. Three turns of herl from a peacock's sword feather to represent the thorax
Hackle: Cock starling neck feather

Pryce Tannatt included this in the personal collection of wet flies which he presented to the Welsh Salmon & Trout Angling Association. He maintained that it took trout on mountain lakes.

This dark brown water beetle (*Velia currens*) has two orange stripes on its back and an orange undercarriage. It is to be found on lakes and slow-flowing rivers like the Teifi in the bog land area of Tregaron.

Whisky Fly
(Albert Whillock)

PLATE 22

Hook: 6, 8 & 10 long shank
Tying silk: Orange
Body: Flat gold tinsel
Rib: Red floss
Hackle: Hot orange
Wing: Orange bucktail or orange squirrel

This pattern is very successful in taking rainbows feeding just below the surface. It comes into its own on most Welsh reservoirs such as Trawsfynydd, Brenig, Eglwys Nunydd and Llandegfedd by about June when the rainbow trout are fairly active and aggressive; and then a fast or a very fast retrieve of the Whisky often attracts them.

The Whisky Fly occasionally is fished on a slow-sinking line in the mid-water levels. It is a fly that does very well in coloured water. On Llyn Brenig it is a particularly good lure once the water has warmed up.

Williams' Favourite

PLATE 19

Hook: 12-14
Tying silk: Black
Tail: Two or three black whisks
Rib: Silver wire

PLATE 14
Edmondson's Welsh Fly, February Red, Felan Fach, Fflambo
Francis' Fly, Grannom, Halford's Grannom, Rhwyfwyr Tinwyrdd
Gravel Bed (Powell), Gravel Bed (Tannatt), Gravel Bed (Ronalds), Gravel Bed (variant)
Green Peter, Greenwell's Glory, Dai's Greenwell, Grenadier

PLATE 15
Grouse & Claret, Grouse & Green, Grouse & Purple, Gwybedyn Bach Traed Cochion
Gwybedyn Bach Llyn Manod, Gwybedyn Bach Du, Hare's Ear, Harry Tom
Haul a Gwynt, Haul a Gwynt (variant), Hawthorn Fly, Hawthorn Fly (black ostrich)
Hawthorn Fly (black wing), Hen Lambed, Silver Invicta, Black Invicta

Body: Black silk body
Hackle: Black

One should not accuse Courtney Williams of bias when he praised this pattern which was created by his father who first tried it out on the Dysynni. Since those days it has travelled far and wide and has travelled well too! Black patterns are pre-eminent in Wales and this is about the best there is.

It is effective fished wet or dry, on lake or on river, for brown trout or sewin. Courtney Williams praised its ability to take trout in coloured water and was of the opinion that black was the best colour from the point of view of visibility in those conditions.

Willow Fly (G.E.M. Skues)

Plate 18

Hook: 14
Tying silk: Orange
Body: Mole fur
Hackle: Rusty dun cock
Wing: Hen blackbird

There is no doubt that this pattern, representing *Leuctra geniculata* and devised by Skues influenced a Willow Fly pattern that has been popular in the Tawe valley. It is the same in all its details except that the Tawe pattern originally involved using the fur of the water rat spun on yellow silk.

Woodcock & Green

Plate 19

Hook: 10 & 12
Tying silk: Green
Tail: Golden pheasant tippets
Rib: Gold wire
Body: Green seal's fur
Hackle: Ginger
Wing: Woodcock wing

The Woodcock series is not widely used in Wales, but there are some anglers who still prefer it to the Mallard or the Teal feathers. Of late, with the sharp increase in the cost of partridge feathers, woodcock feathers have been found useful alternatives.

Woodcock & Mixed

Plate 19

Hook: 10 & 12
Tying silk: Red
Tail: Golden pheasant tippets
Rib: Gold wire
Body: Tail half yellow/top half red
Hackle: Ginger
Wing: Woodcock

This pattern is a favourite with anglers on some of the reservoirs in South Wales. The red and yellow body makes for a most colourful pattern and it is probably better equipped to catch the angler - hence it is used more extensively than other members of the series.

Woodcock & Yellow

Plate 19

Hook: 12
Tying silk: Yellow
Body: Yellow tying silk
Hackle: Ginger
Wing: Woodcock

This is a rather ordinary little fly. It is commonly used just as the water is changing colour. The yellow body probably makes it that little bit more visible to the trout.

Worm Fly

PLATE 22

Hook: Two size 10 hooks in tandem
Tying silk: Black
Tail: Red wool
Body: Peacock herl ribbed with gold wire
Hackle: Coch-a-bon-ddu

Why this lure was called the Worm Fly remains a mystery. It is, in fact, nothing more than two Coch-a bon-ddu flies tied on in tandem. The answer may lie in the method of fishing it, rather as one would fish a running worm.

It is important to ensure that the trace between the two hooks is one hundred per cent safe. The Worm Fly is a lure which can be fished very slowly, on the point of a cast, used with a sinking line. On the Llysyfran Reservoir in West Wales the Worm Fly does well when fished in this manner.

The Worm Fly can also be used as a bob fly when fished from a boat. The extra hook probably helps with hooking and the extra length of the fly also allows the angler the opportunity of keeping it longer in the surface film. It has also proved successful when stripped quickly on a floating line when fished from a boat.

For sewin, the Worm-fly is used as a normal wet fly, cast downriver and allowed to swing down and across with the current. The double hook helps with the hooking of sewin which are notorious for their habit of taking short. In very small sizes, two size 12 hooks, it is a good daytime fly, fished level with the eyes and mouths of shoals of newly-arrived 'school' sewin.

York's Special

PLATE 19

Hook: 8, 10, 12
Tying silk: Black
Tag: Red wool
Rib: Gold wire
Body: Black wool
Hackles: Coch-a-bon-ddu or furnace

York's Special (*Bibio pomonae*) is one of the best bob flies to use on Welsh reservoirs. It first gained its reputation on Llyn Trawsfynydd, primarily among anglers fishing from boats. The 'Yorkie', as it is affectionately called, was introduced to Wales by a man who used to sell fishing tackle in the region. The fly took his surname. It is always fished on the bob: the aim is to keep it in or on the surface of the water. It is a copy of the heather fly (*Bibio pomanae*) which appears on some stillwaters in late summer. The red tag is used to suggest the legs of the heather fly which are a vivid red in the upper sections.

Zulu

PLATE 19

Hook: 12, 10, 8 & 6
Tying silk: Black
Tail or Tag: Red Wool
Rib: Flat silver tinsel
Body: Black seal's fur
Hackle: Two black cock hackles, one palmered down the body, the second tied as head hackle

It is very difficult to know where this pattern originated, though not at all hard to guess at how it derived its name. With the love that Welsh anglers have of black fly patterns, it is a natural choice of fly for Welsh waters.

The Zulu is usually used on the bob position - even in competitive angling. The old anglers who wielded longer rods than are seen today would have had the Zulu dribbling along the surface of the water and, fished thus, it had the ability to raise fish from the deep.

The Zulu is also a sewin fly of considerable repute. Here also, it is used as a bob fly on a three-fly cast. Sometimes the wake that it causes as it skims the surface rouses the sewin, and many anglers claim that, although the fish is often taken on the second fly, it is the bob that has done the work of attracting.

Zulu, Blue

PLATE 19

Hook: 12, 10, 8 & 6
Tying silk: Black
Tag: Red wool
Body: Black seal's fur ribbed with flat silver tinsel
Hackle: Two hackles - one black cock wound through the body and one blue at the head.

Many favour the Blue Zulu to the Black Zulu when fishing for sewin.

Zulu, Gold

PLATE 19

Hook: 10 & 12
Tying silk: Black
Tag: Red wool
Rib: Gold tinsel
Body: Peacock herl
Hackle: One coch-a-bon-ddu palmered down the body.

Many use a gold tinsel for the ribbing and call it the Gold Zulu.

PLATE 16
Orange Invicta, Iron Blue Dun, Acheson's Blue Dun, Robert's Blue Dun
Iron Blue Dun (Glas Cwta), Large Whirling Dun, Usk Light Blue, Little Chap
Llew Bach, Macrel Bach, Mallard & Claret, March Brown
Edmonds' March Brown, Evans' Usk March Brown, March Brown Quill, Marlow Buzz

The Dry Flies

There is a theory, related by David Jacques, that dry fly fishing 'was invented by a company of southern (English) gentlemen to make the capture of trout more difficult in order to display their superiority over less distinguished anglers'. This fails to take into account a rival claim that dry fly angling was, in fact, developed in Cardiganshire - where the Cardis, a tribe famed for their caution, preferred not to let the fly out of their sight!

The dry fly method, especially where the flies are of one's own manufacture, is the most pleasurable and satisfying method. It is often the most productive too. It is, however, a method that seems to have taken longer to come to Wales than elsewhere, though there is every reason to suppose that on the rivers Dee, Wye and Usk the fishing practices which were already widespread throughout England, were in use from the earliest times. Travellers - as well as the landed gentry classes in Wales who had connections in England - were very likely to have brought the dry fly technique to private waters. The pity is that none of them has left us a clear record of it.

Established wet flies like Coch-a-bon-ddu and March Brown were tied with two or three cock hackles and were used as floaters. These early 'dry' flies were expected to sit up well on the water. Their hackle and wings had to give the right outline. Great care was taken with the body material of these flies; the hackle, too, had to be rigid, luminous and bright.

In the comparatively short time from the publication of *Llawlyfr y Pysgotwr* in 1899, where dry flies do not merit a mention, to the present day, Welsh dry fly fishing has taken its proper place in Wales and made many important contributions to the art world-wide.

The main lessons to be learned from the great Welsh dresser-innovators, such as Rev Powell and Dai Lewis, are twofold: meticulous care in the choice of materials; and imagination. There is no doubt that mono-filament nylon, floating plastic lines, braided-butt leaders and fly-floatants have made all the difference in making the dry fly do its job - namely float - but it still requires an artist-craftsman to make the imitation lively and to present it cunningly to the trout.

In recent years, there has been a remarkable 're-discovery' of the dry fly as a formidable method of taking trout on stillwaters. This is particularly the case on those hot, still days of high summer when the fish are completely unimpressed by the wet fly technique. In such inauspicious angling conditions it is often those who have assembled a team of dries who have managed to catch fish when others fail.

PLATE 17
Dai's Nailer, Usk Nailer, Oak Fly, Old Joe
Old Warrior, Orl, Red Palmer, Black Palmer,
Badger (Grizzly) Palmer, Parry's Black Spider, Partridge & Black, Peter Ross
Pheasant Tail, Pluen Rhen Law, Poacher, Pupil Teacher

Plate 18
Big Sedge, Small Sedge, Teal-wing Sedge, Green-ringed Sedge
Smokey Blue, Stone Fly, Stone Fly (Scotcher), Stone Fly (Parry)
Dark Stone, Roger Woolley, Willow Fly, Snipe (variant)
Teal & Green, Teal & Black, Teal Blue & Silver, Teal & Red

Badger, Black

PLATE 24

Hook: 16 & 18
Tying silk: Black
Body: Black silk
Hackle: Small badger

All small Badger flies are popular with Welsh anglers who like to fish up the smaller rivers during high summer.

The high-visibility quality of Badger flies is important and there are considerable differences of opinion on the amount of white that should be used in the hackle. Some feel the white should represent about fifty per cent of the hackle, while others require just the tips of the hackle to be white. In recent years the Black Badger has been on the ascendant both on river and lake. Some use it during a buzzer rise and fish it semi-dry in the surface film.

Badger, Red

PLATE 24

Hook: 16 & 18
Tying silk: Red
Body: Red seal's fur
Hackle: Small badger

Badger, Yellow

PLATE 24

Hook: 12-14
Tying silk: Black
Body: Yellow body
Rib: Gold wire
Hackle: Well-marked badger cock

The Yellow Badger, on account of its excellent visibility, is the firm favourite of the Badger series.

Brookes' Fancy

PLATE 26

Hook: 13 & 14
Tying silk: Purple
Body: Purple floss ribbed with peacock herl
Hackle: Off-white

This grayling fly was originally tied by a well known postman from Ludlow. Brookes, an inventive fly dresser, used it mainly on the river Teme. It was then used on the Severn and earned a considerable reputation there. It has also been used on the few stretches of the Teifi that hold grayling.

Coachman, Hackle

PLATE 12

Hook: 10, 12 & 14
Tying silk: Brown
Body: Peacock herl
Hackle: White cock in front with ginger cock supporting it

This dry version of the Coachman is often used on the rough streams of Wales because of its visibility, a quality which is an advantage on dark days and in the gathering darkness of evening against the western sky.

Cobbler

PLATE 23

Hook: 10 & 12
Tying silk: Yellow
Tail: Ginger hackle fibres
Body: Dirty yellow wool
Rib: Gold wire

The old shoe-shop at Pontrhydfendigaid was an extremely interesting place - a centre for many community activities, not the least of which was flytying. David Jones, known as 'Dai Cobbler', was a man whose approach to fishing was unorthodox but highly effective. He tied his dry flies for one purpose only and that was *visibility*. He maintained that patterns in the upper reaches of rivers were not over-important.

His flies were big by conventional standards and some of his four-hackled flies, tied on number ten hooks, were virtually unsinkable.

They would hop, skip and jump down the running sections of the river. A light ginger hackle is highly visible, even in peat-stained water. Dai Cobbler would often tie half-a-dozen flies before he went out.

Dai Cobbler, irrespective of conditions and weather, would use his heavily-hackled dry fly in the quickest of runs and would strike at the slightest suggestion of a disturbance near the fly. He did not believe in playing a fish; and as soon as the fish was hooked, it was bounced unceremoniously along the surface until it was on dry land.

Dai's Alder

PLATE 23

Hook: 12
Tying silk: Black
Body: Peacock herl
Hackle: Two black cocks
Front hackle: Grouse feather

The Alder is regarded as an important dry fly for the summer months on the upper sections of the river Teifi. This insect (*Sialis lutaria*), with its large black head, dark thorax and heavily-marked brown wings, is easily recognisable and its appearance meant that anglers would immediately fish Dai's Alder in its dry form.

The story of its creation is an interesting one. A collier by the name of Dan Jones used to buy flies at Cardiff and then take them to his home water in the Teifi valley to experiment with and amaze the locals. On one occasion he brought an Alder fly with

him and, immediately his friend Dai Lewis saw it, he set about modifying it.

Dai Lewis had little time for winged flies - and so the wing on the Alder was replaced with a hackle from the grouse body. This hackle was wound in front of the two black hackles. The overall fly was of generous proportions and was an excellent floater. Sometimes Dai would substitute dark ginger hackle for the black one; but this adaptation would often depend on the quality of the hackle available - not so much on the technical requirements of the pattern.

Dan's Supreme

PLATE 23

Hook: 12
Tying silk: Yellow
Body: Yellow hind portion. Mole fur front portion
Hackle: Rusty dun

Dan Jones, like many Welsh country men and boys, had to go 'down to South Wales' to find employment in the coal mines in the twenties. His heart never left the Upper Teifi valley: he was passionately fond of fishing. He devised the 'Supreme' as a result of his stock of excellent blue hackles derived from his expertise at the cock fighting pit. The best fighting cocks came from Pembrokeshire where they were known as Pembrokeshire Blues. In the course of his cockfighting exploits, Dan had been able to collect some very special cock hackles.

His Supreme is a fly with excellent visibility and buoyancy.

Doctor

PLATE 23

Hook: 14
Tying silk: Black
Tag: Rabbit flax having been dyed in picric

acid to make it yellow
Hackle: Two small coch-a-bon-ddu cock hackles

It has been suggested that the Doctor is a pattern created to represent one of the many beetles that are found on the rivers in summer. There is no doubt that the Doctor fulfils this role but it is also an all-round pattern that is worth having in one's box to try when the trout are proving difficult to please.

This is one of the best patterns to use on the upper Teifi in the post-grannom period. The trout on the Teifi tend to feed heavily during the grannom hatches and become rather difficult to tempt immediately after. Rev Edward Powell on his visits to Tregaron used this pattern to good effect. In his later years Powell dressed the pattern with a smaller hackle.

Dogsbody

PLATE 23

Hook: 12 14 & 16
Tying silk: Brown
Tail: Three strands of tail of cock pheasant
Rib: Oval gold
Body: Camel-coloured dog's hair
Hackle: Barred Plymouth Rock, with red cock's hackle in front

One of the best dry flies to come from the Usk. It is regarded as a general purpose dry fly with some similarity to the Rough Olive and the hackled Hare's Ear; yet many anglers believe that it is a representation of the sand fly. According to the story, the late Harry Powell, fly- and hair-dresser of Usk, was sent, by post, an order from an angler in North Wales, for a dozen flies, the pattern for which was enclosed in the envelope. The body of the pattern proved difficult to match, being of an elusive camel shade. The problem was later solved when a farmer

came into Harry's shop for a haircut. At his heels was a dog. The dog's coat was the precise and identical shade that Harry had been hunting! While his assistant went about the business of giving the farmer a haircut, Harry set about collecting the required hair from the dog. The pattern was thus baptised.

Ermine Moth

PLATE 23

Hook: 12 & 14
Tying silk: Black
Tag: Yellowish orange wool
Rib: Thick black cotton
Body: White wool
Hackle: Two grey partridge

A great favourite with Rev Edward Powell. There is no doubt, however, that the pattern was in existence long before the Rev gentleman developed it. The vicar was responsible for adding the tag to the original.

The body is tied full with wool, the black cotton being prominent between the segments of the body. The small grey partridge hackle feathers are found in small numbers on the breast of the bird. To find the right feather, it is advisable to buy a fully feathered (dead) bird from a game dealer. Store carefully the small feathers from the mid-back and the mid-chest regions, as they are really valuable and in short supply.

The Ermine Moth is tied with two soft partridge hackles, tied back to back, thus making the hackle stand upright. The dynamics of the hackle fibres assist buoyancy. Some tie in a white cock hackle to support the partridge.

The Ermine Moth has developed into an evening pattern, but it should not be neglected during the day. It is said that there was a time, on the Teifi, when the

PLATE 19

Teal & Mixed, Teifi Pools Sedge, Troellwr (Corff Llygoden Ddwr), Troellwr Mawr (Dafis)
Troellwr Mawr (Owen), Dark Snipe & Purple, Snipe & Yellow, Usk Dark Blue
Snipe & Purple
Usk Purple, Water Cricket, Williams' Favourite, Woodcock & Yellow
Woodcock & Green, Woodcock & Mixed, York's Special
Zulu, Blue Zulu, Gold Zulu

signal to put it on was the ten o'clock train which used to run on the track adjoining the river. The visibility of the Ermine Moth during the final thirty minutes was responsible for the downfall of many a trout.

Greenwell

PLATE 23

Hook: 12 & 14
Tying silk: Yellow
Rib: Gold wire
Body: Yellow silk waxed (Cobbler's wax)
Hackle: Coch-a-bon-ddu cock or Greenwell cock (Ginger and black)

On the fast-flowing Welsh rivers little use is made of the original winged Greenwell. The dry fly used in Wales carries two, three or even four hackles. The version of the Greenwell, made for the upper Teifi by Charles Harries was dressed on this principle.

Although, in the early part of the season, anglers favour the darker version of the Greenwell dressed with the coch-a-bon-ddu hackle, as the season progresses, the lighter coloured hackle of the Greenwell (black and ginger) is preferred. Most dry-fly anglers on Welsh rivers cast the dry fly into the neck of a pool and let it ride the broken water. When olives are in evidence the Greenwell is a favoured pattern.

Grey Duster

PLATE 23

Hook: 12 & 14
Tying silk: Brown
Body: Blue rabbit fur
Hackle: Well marked badger

The river Dee in North Wales and its tributaries, the Ceiriog and the Alwen, have been an important nursery school for dry-fly anglers. This has resulted in a number of fly patterns being evolved in those valleys which have proved their value on other fisheries in Wales. Among them is the Grey Duster. It is difficult to say what insect the Grey Duster is intended to represent. It could be an imitation of a member of the Perlidae family, like the February red, willow fly, the needle fly or even a moth. Some maintain that it is one of those all-rounders that are capable of taking the dry-fly angler right through the season.

The Grey Duster is a very easy fly to tie, but it is important to have the right colour for the body. Rabbit fur has three distinct colours. The top layer of guard fibres is brownish, the intermediate layer is fawn and the lower layer is a blue dun colour. This latter is the colour required for the Grey Duster.

Grizzly Dun

PLATE 23

Hook: 14
Tying silk: Yellow
Tail: Grizzle fibres
Body: Well waxed yellow silk
Hackle: Light grizzle grey badger hackle

This fly gained its reputation on the rivers of mid Wales and the upper reaches of the Wye. It can be fished wet or dry, and does very well when the olives are about. Its advantage is that it is highly visible and, as such, is often put on when the light conditions become difficult.

The Grizzly Dun is also worthy of a try on lakes: it did once score well on Llyn Tarw near Caersws. Llyn Tarw is a unique fishery in that the introduced brook trout now breed there naturally and at times they can offer amazing sport.

Imperial

PLATE 23

Hook: 13 & 14
Tying silk: Purple
Tail: Dun fibres
Rib: Gold wire
Body: Heron herl
Hackle: Honey dun

Oliver Kite, creator of this pattern, was an angler of exceptional ability. He came to fish the upper Teifi in March 1963. Skirting each pool was a crust of ten-week-old ice after the abnormally hard winter and daily, from this harsh environment, Oliver Kite took trout of excellent quality on the dry fly.

The fly that did the trick was his newly-created Imperial - his representation of the early spring olive. Early spring olives hatch every day, even in that sort of weather, and Kite, having studied the natural, produced a first attempt imitation tied with green silk and a light ginger hackle. By the end of the week it had been modified, with the purple silk showing through the heron herl which had been doubled over in order to form a thorax. The hackle was of a dark dun.

John Storey

PLATE 26

Hook: 14 & 16
Tying silk: Claret
Body: Peacock herl
Hackle: Medium dark red cock
Wing: Tip of speckled feather from mallard breast

Eric Horsfall Turner had a great knowledge of the river Severn in mid-Wales. He took many fish with his own patented dry flies and with the wet fly fished upriver. He very much liked this John Storey fly pattern from Yorkshire, where he himself spent some years as town clerk of Scarborough. It is claimed that the pattern was devised by a John Storey who was riverkeeper from the Ryedales Angling Club.

Dry-fly fishing during the months of November and December under grey, dull skies can impose considerable strain on the grayling angler's eyesight. A well-marked wing on a very small pattern is of great help in this respect - and John Storey is one of the most visible of patterns.

Ke-he

Hook: 10 & 12
Tying silk: Claret
Tail: Red tag on golden pheasant tippets
Body: Peacock herl
Hackle: Ginger or brown

Some anglers in Wales use the normal Ke-he pattern as a dry fly for grayling. Grayling will sometimes take the Black Ke-he in preference to the standard dressing above.

Leslie Peters' Special

PLATE 23

Hook: 12 & 14
Tying silk: Yellow
Whisks: Honey dun
Body: Orange and natural wool mixed with tying silk visible through body
Hackle: Honey dun (tied parachute style)

The river Usk is an ideal river for dry-fly fishing. Of pool and riffle nature with ideal glides and runs, it is a river where the dry-fly angler can drop his offering with ease and with reasonable expectation of results.

On glides on the river Usk this parachute fly is ideal - in that it fishes close on the water and has the advantage of no protruding hackle in the surface film. The parachute, although having many advocates in Wales, is certainly confined to particular localities, the Usk being the chief of them.

PLATE 20
Ace of Spades, Baby Doll
Badger Matuka, Black Lure
Cenhinen Tony

PLATE 21
Black Dog Nobbler
Jersey Herd, Jack Frost
Muddler Minnow, Missionary

The parachute style of dressing the hackle of a dry fly is an old one that seems to have lost much favour in the last two decades on most Welsh rivers. A couple of years ago Brian Clarke and John Goddard resurrected the principle with their film and book promoting the USD Paraduns. Their novel approach to an old theme had the hackle below the hook, which allowed for very delicate presentation and confronts the trout with a dimpled silhouette.

March Brown *(Dai Lewis)*

PLATE 23

Hook: 13
Tying silk: Brown
Tail: Ginger whisks
Rib: Yellow thread
Body: Hare's ear
Hackles: Ginger hackle with two brown partridge in front

Dai Lewis achieved considerable success with his dry fly patterns. This dry March Brown is another superb example. It is dressed rather full with a bulky, bushy hackle. This pattern is highly visible and a good floater, ideally suited for fishing quick-flowing water in mid-summer.

The March brown hatches on rivers like the Usk and the Teifi can extend over quite a long period - thus explaining the durability of this pattern for most of the season. It is conceivable that in late summer the dry March Brown could be taken by the trout for the August dun.

Orange Otter

PLATE 26

Hook: 16 & 18
Tying silk: Orange
Tail: Red cock
Body: Pale biscuit colour underpart of an otter's throat, soaked in picric acid solution and then boiled in the same solution for a few minutes - plus equal volume of red ink, plus an equal amount of water (original dressing!)
Hackle: Wound around the middle of the hook, thus dividing the body in half

Devised by the late Rev Edward Powell. His patterns are all immensely difficult to tie because of the complex nature of the body material. He found a lot of use for picric acid. His patterns are always worth the trouble, provided one can get them tied with the good substitute materials.

This pattern, known by its initials O.O., is probably one of the best grayling patterns of all. Anglers have been constantly amazed at its power to get the grayling to come up and strike at it. Its creator was known also to have used it for trout fishing in September.

Paragon *(Dai Lewis)*

PLATE 24

Hook: 12 & 14
Tying silk: Brown
Tail: Three or four strands of dark red cock
Body: Rabbit face
Hackle: Two Rhode Island hen, dark chocolate colour, ten turns

This dry fly was a great favourite with anglers on the upper Teifi who went out fishing in the late evening. It was made popular after Vicar Powell advised Courtney Williams about it, who in turn included it in his book, the ever-popular *A Dictionary of Trout Flies*. Its usefulness in the late evening as a sedge imitation earned it its name - which implies perfection.

Dai Lewis, who first tied this fly, although a great believer in top quality cock hackles for dry-fly patterns, recommended the softer, more hairy hen hackle for his sedge representation: the reason being that he dressed his Sedge flies in order to fish them predominantly in slack water.

The two hackles are placed back-to-back. The natural curve of the hackles forms a compact unit, and the hen fibres, on contact with the surface of the water, bend and thus form a good base for the fly to sit on.

This is a late-season sedge imitationand it works best after hot summer days in July and August.

Pheasant Tail

PLATE 24

Hook: 14
Tying silk: Hot orange
Tail: Two or three strands of honey dun
Rib: Gold wire
Body: Two strands of rich-coloured, ruddy fibres from the centre of feather of a cock pheasant tail
Hackle: Rusty dun cock

This is one of the most under-rated flies for use in Wales. In its dry form it probably represents the spinners of some of the *Ephemera* family. Much has been written about the blue-winged olive and many have been the debates about the best artificial to tempt the fish when they are feeding on it. On the Teifi the Pheasant Tail will outstrip the renowned Orange Quill when the sherry spinners are about.

Dry-fly fishers on the middle reaches of the Teifi insist on having a very dark dun hackle. One of the excellent dry-fly anglers of the area, a certain Danny Pryse, would swear by the dark Pheasant Tail - 'swear' being the operative word! He would use his dry flies in the necks of the pools and expect his flies to hop-scotch their way over the broken water where the big trout lurked in the warm days of summer.

Red Tag

PLATE 26

Hook: 10 & 12
Tying silk: Black
Tag: Red wool
Rib: Gold wire
Body: Peacock herl
Hackle: Red cock hackle

This a very old fly pattern - going back some hundred and fifty years. It was first used in Wales as a trout fly - with the addition of the red tag to the normal Coch-a-bon-ddu pattern.

It is as a grayling fly that the Red Tag is really outstanding. It is used on the river Dee in the Corwen area and there it takes grayling in either the wet or dry form. When the river is low, and after a November frost, the best fun is had with it in its dry form.

Severn Ke

PLATE 26

Hook: 16 & 18
Tying silk: Claret
Tail: Red fluorescent wool on golden pheasant tippets
Body: Peacock herl
Hackle: White cock

This pattern, used by a few Llanidloes anglers on certain sections of the upper Severn, is an adaptation of the Ke-he fly which is popular in the Orkneys. The use of the white hackle has been a great advantage when fishing in late Autumn under poor light conditions. Some keen grayling anglers tie this pattern in two distinct styles. When confronted with swift-flowing water they use much larger versions on hooks size 12 and they use two hackles. In slack and calm waters they use a very lightly dressed version with only one or two turns of hackle.

PLATE 22
Black Muddler, White Muddler
Sweeny Todd
Worm Fly, Whisky Fly

PLATE 23
Dai's Alder, Cobbler, Dan's Supreme, Doctor
Dogsbody, Ermine Moth, Greenwell
Grey Duster, Grizzly Dun, Imperial,
March Brown, Leslie Peters' Special

Small Harry

PLATE 24

Hook: 12
Tying silk: Black
Tail: Red cock fibres
Body: Rabbit face
Rib: Yellow thread
Hackles: Red cock hackle with partridge brown in front

Used as a dry version of the March Brown, the Small Harry is dressed rather full with plenty of turns of the red cock. Sometimes two cock hackles are used. The dry version of the March Brown is used on Usk and Teifi when water flows are low and fishing the wet March Brown is difficult.

Sun fly

PLATE 24

Hook: 10, 12 & 14
Tying silk: Black
Body: Rabbit forehead
Hackles: Two coch-a-bon-ddu and a cree

This pattern was tied very full by its creator, the late Dai Lewis of Tregaron. He tied his flies without the aid of a vice, and all his patterns had that 'living' quality. Body fur, taken from the forehead of a rabbit, gave the fly an overall dark appearance. Cree hackle was used to give the fly a sparkle. It is difficult today to appreciate how effective some of these big floating flies were. One of the bigger patterns tied on a number ten hook would be cast into the neck of a broken run and it would come bouncing down like a ping-pong ball with the flow.

Sun Fly, Baby

PLATE 24

Hook: 14 & 16
Tying silk: Black
Tail: Three strands of coch-a-bon-ddu
Body: Rabbit's face fur ribbed with tying silk
Hackle: Very small coch-a-bon-ddu

This pattern represents the black gnat. Unlike its bigger bother, it is effective during the early days of the season; and it has lost its effectiveness by mid summer.

Treacle Parkin

PLATE 26

Hook: 12 & 14
Tying silk: Yellow
Tail: Yellow/Orange wool
Body: Peacock herl
Hackle: Dark red/brown

Grayling anglers disagree about the colour of the tag on this pattern. Some favour the bright yellow above the orange yellow shade. Grayling are not quite as concerned with the merits and de-merits of these various shades!

Most serious grayling anglers believe that after the grayling has refused a particular pattern it is advisable to change to something totally different. Treacle Parkin is ideal for this ploy and success will often follow a change of fly.

The Treacle Parkin originated in Yorkshire where it is a favoured fly. Flies often undergo modification when they travel but, with the exception of the odd grayling angler using coch-a-bon-ddu hackle instead of the dark red/brown as on the original, Treacle Parkin has remained unaltered.

Welshman's Button

PLATE 24

Hook: 12
Tying silk: Brown
Body: Peacock herl
Hackle: Coch-a-bon-ddu, or red game and black game mixed

This is the traditional Welsh dressing of the Welshman's Buttton, tied by Tom Tom in mid-Wales. He would dress it very full, with seven to ten turns of the hackle. Welsh anglers have always regarded the Welshman's Button as a beetle imitation.

Courtney Williams maintains that the Welshman's Button was a term derived from Welshman's Butty. 'Butty' is an expression used among colliers in the South Wales valleys for a friend. Many claim that the beetle which the Welshman's Button represents, *Sericostoma personatum*, is not all that common in Wales.

A pattern still used on the reservoirs of South Wales is one designed by Eric Taverner:

Hook: 12 or 14
Tying silk: Crimson
Body: Peacock herl (greenish)
Hackle: Black cock
Wing-case: Ginger feather from partridge tail

Welsh Partridge

PLATE 24

Hook: 12 & 14
Tying silk: Claret
Tail: Two strands from partridge tail
Body: Claret seal's fur
Hackle: Claret hackle with three turns of partridge hackle in front

Courtney Williams, the creator of this fly, claims the Welsh Partridge to be an outstanding dry fly that is capable of taking fish on any river other than the chalk-streams. This has proved to be a fair claim for a pattern which is at its best at the latter end of the trout season.

Courtney Williams says that some of his friends found the Welsh Partridge a useful wet fly but there is no doubt that its primary role is that of a dry fly.

Small dry flies are often difficult to see. The Welsh Partridge should be dressed with a grey speckled partridge breast feather (as opposed to a back one) this makes the fly more visible - especially when the light is poor.

Whiskers

PLATE 24

Hook: 10, 12 & 14
Tying silk: Red
Rib: Gold wire
Body: Dark red wool or seal's fur
Hackles: Two or three ginger cocks, tied palmered

It is hard to imagine what these balls of fur and feathers are taken for. Some of the bigger patterns resemble nothing other than miniature feather dusters. Yet they are effective. It was once thought that they worked best at dusk when the moths were about, but they can be equally effective during daytime too, representing, as some believe, the hairy caterpillars, known in Wales as 'Sioni blewog' (Hairy Johnnies) that get onto the water from time to time.

The only difference between the Whiskers pattern used in North Wales and the one used in the Usk area is that on the Usk it is ribbed with flat gold.

Witch, Rolt's

PLATE 26

Hook: 14 & 16
Tying silk: Black
Tail: Red wool
Body: Peacock herl
Hackle: Honey dun

This was the original of the Witch series, created by H.A. Rolt whose expertise in grayling fishing is recorded in his book, *Grayling Fishing in South County Streams*. Most of the grayling patterns in the Witch series have followed the principle set by Rolt in this prototype - a small, thick-set body with plenty of red in the dressing.

Witch, Silver

PLATE 26

Hook: 14 & 16
Tying silk: Black
Tail: Red wool
Body: Peacock herl
Hackle: Badger cock (palmered)

A variation on the White Witch (see below). Best as a dry fly.

Witch, White

PLATE 26

Hook: 14 & 16
Tying silk: Black
Tail: Red wool
Body: Peacock herl
Hackle: White cock tied palmer fashion

The Witch patterns can be fished either as dry or wet flies. The White Witch does, however, do far better when fished upriver in its dry state. It is particularly useful on the Wye and Dee rivers.

Yellow Sally

PLATE 24

Hook: 14
Tying silk: Yellow
Body: Pale yellow wool
Hackle: Yellow cock hackle (dyed)

The yellow sally (*Isoperla grammatica*) is a member of the stone-fly family and, although quite common and easily recognised by anglers, it is not a favourite with the trout. The small yellow sally (*Chloroperla torrentium*) is, however, found in considerable numbers in the upper reaches of many Welsh rivers and at times the trout rise to them quite freely. Trout generally take the female just as it is ovipositing or in its spent form.

PLATE 24
Paragon, Pheasant Tail, Small Harry
Sun Fly, Baby Sun Fly
Welshman's Button, Welsh Partridge, Whiskers
Yellow Badger, Black Badger, Red Badger
Yellow Sally

The Sewin Flies

The sewin flies used by Welsh anglers at the beginning of the nineteenth century were very similar to those used for trout fishing. The reason for this thinking was the belief that the sewin was biologically similar to the brown trout. George Agar Hansard writing about his fishing in different parts of Wales in the year 1834 noted that the best fly for sewin was a Red Fly, which was also used for trout fishing. This Red Fly was probably used as an imitation of the February red. His advice on the make-up of the Red Fly was:

> 'Take a weak light and yellowish brown dun hen feather, either from the neck or any part of the body; wind two or three times close together, a little below the shank of the hook, and make the body clear below it, of a mixture of ruddy black sheep wool, mingled with orange; use yellow silk to rib up the body with it'.

It was to be dressed on a big hook, preferably No.5. The fly to be used as a dropper for sewin fishing was made thus:

> 'A light blue hen or cock hackle with two or three turns round the top of the shank of the hook, with a body below of a mixture of light orange wool and a little dark fur with yellow tips from a hare's ear ribbed with gold thread'.

If the water ran heavy it was further recommended to put on wings made of spotted galino fowl or a grouse speckled feather. Even in those early days Hansard underlines the quality of the Welsh sewin and advises:

'...use good sound gut for your bottom, for they are very strong
and yield nobble sport'.

This principle of using over-grown trout flies for sewin has persisted in Wales
from those early days until the last couple of decades. Flies like the colourful
Dunkeld, Alexandra, Zulu, Butcher and Peter Ross dressed on number eight
hooks were the accepted sewin flies.

Fortunately, Hugh Falkus in his seminal book, *Seatrout Fishing*, 1962,
challenged this principle and brought about a necessary change. Thereafter,
sewin flies have undoubtedly taken on a new look.

Unlike most other fish, the sewin's reaction to the artificial fly depends a
lot on the length of time that particular sewin being fished for has been in
the river. The longer the sewin remains in the river, the more difficult it
becomes to catch it. The big colourful lures are not necessarily effective for
these fish. It is noticeable that, unlike salmon or brown trout flies, some
sewin flies are effective in one section of a river but conspicuously not in
another.

Sewin fly fishing can be divided into two distinct categories: Daylight
fishing with water levels varying from high to low. Night fishing when the
water level is medium to low.

Daytime fishing for sewin demands the use of smaller flies and, on the
whole fairly sober colours. If the water is running down after a flood with a
little bit of colour in it, then silver-bodied, colourful flies can be effective.
Bigger flies can also be used when the water flow is above normal. Many fly
patterns have been specifically developed in Wales to fish for sewin during the
day and most of them are made of dubbing bodies with blue dun hackles.

Night fly fishing for sewin demands a different sort of fly. Most night-time
sewin flies have *silver* bodies or marked colour patterns and they are often of
bigger dimensions. Night fishing has become extremely popular in Wales and
is probably more widely practised here than anywhere else in Britain. There
are some rivers in the Principality which offer some of the very finest sewin
fishing, and the Welsh approach to the sport is becoming a very organised
and sophisticated one.

Many trends in seatrout fishing have been started in Wales: in recent
seasons, the use of hair wings. Wings composed of hair give a far better
colour pattern and more life in the deep, still pools and glides. The latest
trend on several Welsh rivers is to construct flies of far longer dimensions:
tandem, terror and tube flies of three and four inches long are not
uncommon. These long flies, in many respects similar to reservoir lures,

PLATE 25
Amber Nymph, Amber Nymph (Sweet), Black Buzzer
Corixa, Corixa (Brett), Emyr's Fancy
Hare's Ear Nymph, Ken's Grey Midge, March Brown Nymph
March Brown Nymph (variant), Longhorn

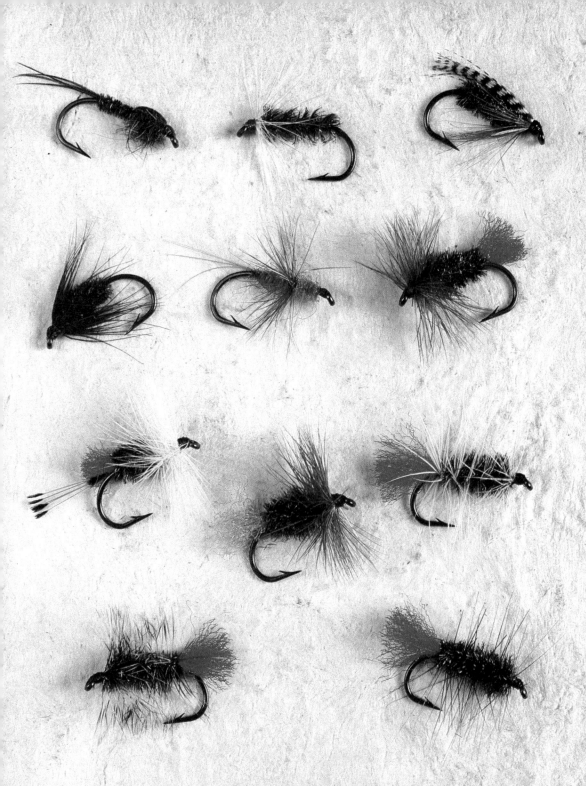

PLATE 26
Pheasant Tail Nymph, Brookes' Fancy, John Storey
Kill Devil Spider, Orange Otter, Red Tag
Severn Ke, Treacle Parkin, White Witch
Silver Witch, Rolt's Witch

require special fishing methods. Slow and fast stripping, varying the movement of the lure, all these tactics are used on dark summer nights.

It is also of interest to learn that the use of surface flies is on the increase on Welsh rivers and that some of the old traditional floating patterns are regaining favour. Why the big sewin that has ignored all kinds of flies and lures that have been swimming past his nose for hours will suddenly rise from the deep to take a fly moving on the surface is beyond one's comprehension. It is such imponderables that make dressing flies for sewin - and fishing them - so fascinating.

Alexandra

PLATE 1

Hook: 6, 8 & 10, tandem and as tube
Tying silk: Black
Body: Flat silver, ribbed with silver wire
Hackle: Black hen
Wing: Green herl from sword tail of peacock. A thin strip of red swan feather along each side
Cheeks: Small jungle cock each side

Anglers either love this pattern or hate it. There was a time when it was outlawed from certain lakes because of its killing powers. No such reputation surrounds it today. Yet in the jungle cock form it is a good lure for early season rainbows.

It is gaining stature yearly as a sewin fly and has adjusted well to its metamorphosis as a tube fly. The green peacock sword feathers give it a very attractive action and the silver body and black feathers with a red stripe give it a good colour pattern.

The Alexandra is often used in smaller sizes as a trout fly on rivers. It is effective when the water is coloured, and is often accused of taking undersized trout and parr. Very few of our stillwaters today are not subjected to artificial stocking from hatcheries and a truly wild brown trout fishery is becoming a rarity. Such a wild trout fishery is Claerwen and often a small Alexandra can be most effective even on days when the coch-a-bon-ddu is hatching in its thousands.

This royal fly, named after Princess Alexandra, was reputedly created by a Dr Brunton - although some maintain that W.G. Turle of Stockbridge was responsible for it. It is at least 130 years old. It is primarily a sewin fly, especially when a little jungle cock is added to it and it is tied as a tandem or a tube fly.

Allrounder

PLATE 1

Hook: 6 or 8
Tying silk: Black
Tail: Golden pheasant toppings
Body: Black seal's fur
Rib: Silver thread
Hackle: Black cock
Wing: Black squirrel with overlay of red squirrel
Topping: Peacock sword feathers
Cheeks: Jungle cock

This fly has all the ingredients of traditional sewin flies rolled into one and is the basic tool of a night session for sewin.

The river Rheidol has a run of very big sewin in late May and early June and this pattern has proved effective on many a night. Although the popular sizes are six and eight it has been discovered that the big sewin, after being in the river for a long time, favour the smaller sizes.

I received a copy of this fly from Illtyd Griffiths - a great sewin angler. Later, I received a letter from the Tawe Valley and it seems that the pattern was devised by Terry Graham from Clydach. He also added tippets to the tail. The fly was widely used by Terry in the sixties. It is also a very good salmon fly.

An identical pattern - but minus the red squirrel section of the wing - has been used for a long time on the river Taf in Carmarthenshire and Pembrokeshire. The Taf compares favourably with any other river in Wales for sewin and on the Gynin, a major tributary of the Taf, the Allrounder has produced some impressive bags.

A useful variant of the Allrounder was developed with success on the Towy in the summer of 1983, a particularly difficult season with high temperatures and low-water conditions throughout the prime months of July and August. It was as follows:

the tying as out-lined above, with the exception of the jungle cock cheeks. For these, substitute a dark muddler (deer-hair) head and fish as a surface-lure or in the surface film. After some use the fly will tend to sink out of the surface levels; when this occurs, and takes are observed to fall-off, a little floatant should be applied - to a dry specimen - to assist buoyancy.

Blackie

PLATE 1

Hook: Tandem, two number 4 or 6. A number 4 plus a number 6 double
Tying silk: Black
Rib: Silver wire
Body: Black seal's fur or black floss
Hackle: Black cock
Wing: Black squirrel
Cheek: Jungle cock

The Blackie is a lure that has transferred from reservoir to river fishing in recent times.

This big lure is used when the sewin are lying deep, hugging the river bed. Sinking lines should be employed to take it down to secure that eye-level confrontation with the quarry. It works well deep down, after midnight.

A survey of recent progress in sewin fishing reveals that the tendency is to use bigger and bigger lures on sunken lines. As in other forms of flyfishing, black seems to be the colour most often productive of results, especially in dark and cold conditions.

The fact that many regular reservoir anglers come to Wales annually to fish for sewin has meant that they bring with them reservoir techniques and tackle. The casting out of long lines and stripping lures back in double-quick time has been one technique that has proved successful with sewin on rivers like the Ystwyth. The Blackie in its

tandem form or on a number six hook with a flying treble has proved very successful in this way.

Two anglers who regularly fish Draycote reservoir near Rugby have employed this approach on the Dwyfawr and, the Blackie has not only done well when stripped quickly on a fast-sinking line, but also when stripped quickly just under the surface of the water on a slow-sinking or intermediate line. This method is especially productive in the early part of the season.

Blue, Black & Silver

PLATE 1

Hook: 4, 6, 8 & 10
Tying silk: Black
Rib: Silver wire
Body: Silver tinsel
Hackle: Blue or black
Wing: Black, blue and natural squirrel hair

The many versions of this pattern are the pack-horses of sewin fishing in Wales. The silver body is the basic requirement and the variations follow the choice of dark and light coloured wings. The Blue, Black & Silver used in Wales is similar to the patterns suggested by Hugh Falkus in his book, *Sea-trout Fishing*. The hair wing has replaced the fibre wngs recommended by Falkus because the hair wing is instantly responsive to the slightest whim of water current as the fly is worked through a pool.

Although variations of colour are largely a matter of personal fancy, the fish do sometimes respond better to a darker or lighter pattern. It would seem that the black wing works better in those rivers which tend to have dark, peat-stained water: the Teifi and the Conway. The light wing works better on rivers with clearer waters like the Aeron and the Ystwyth. The light factor on particular nights also plays an important part.

These variants can either be tied on tube

or treble hooks. John Mercer, a seasoned angler on the river Towy, has cut it so fine as to be seen using just the silver body and black squirrel wing. So long as the resulting over-all fly, including the treble, is an inch and a half in length and fished mainly on a sink-tip line, colour of wings is immaterial. Another angler, Gwyndaf Evans, on the river Rheidol, a dedicated man who certainly seems to spend more time on the river bank than he does in bed during the sewin season, uses a similar fly - but adds two jungle cock eyes as a refinement. These anglers, and many others, have impressive results to testify to the excellence of the Blue, Black & Silver.

Blue, Black & Silver Squirrel

PLATE 1

Hook: 6 & 8
Tying silk: Black
Tail: Tippets or toppings
Rib: Silver thread
Body: Black floss
Hackle: Blue
Wing: Grey squirrel

This version of the Blue, Black & Silver is known as the Squirrel in some areas. The grey squirrel wing makes for a much lighter colour pattern and this sometimes triggers off a response from the sewin on difficult nights, those nights that really test a fly pattern. The simple change of colour of the wing is often enough to give success.

The wing is tied on at a very flat angle over the blue hackle, some even putting the wing under the hackle. The hackle then is tied rather heavily which results in more movement of the hair fibres as the fly is worked through the water. This version works well in dry summers, and on those clear nights with an uncomfortable amount of moonlight. A good fly on the rivers Rheidiol and the Aeron.

Brown Bomber

PLATE 1

Hook: 6 & 8
Tying silk: Brown
Tag: Silver thread
Body: Peacock quill
Hackle: Woodcock (hen blackbird subst.)

Some flies have a killer look about them and this is certainly true of the Brown Bomber, named after heavyweight boxer Jou Louis. The Brown Bomber is another creation from the work-bench of a carpenter on the Dynevor Estate in Llandeilo, the colourful Will Harry. Folklore has it that at one time Lord Dynevor had a stuffed bittern in a glass case in the library at Dynevor Castle, where Will Harry, during one of his Lordship's absences in London, was doing some maintenance work. Always interested in birds, especially dead ones, Will Harry immediately took a fancy to the bittern. A small secret door was ingeniously constructed near the base of the glass case, through which one feather was taken to tie a particular pattern. The pattern proved so successful that another and another, then another feather disappeared out through the trap door. Eventually a half-bald bird revealed a mysterious affliction, and the butler had the bird thrown out before his Lordship discovered the grand larceny.

Flydressers like Wil Harry went to great lengths to secure the correct materials, and the original wing for the Brown Bomber was said not to be a bittern, but the wing of a hen blackbird taken in the third week of January! This piece of information comes from Major T.E. Hughes of Llandeilo, one of the most experienced Towy anglers, who claims to have baptised the fly which his old friend Wil Harry concocted.

Night fishing for sewin is a branch of angling widely practised in West Wales, especially on the river Towy. Some of these patterns, created by local artisans given the privilege of fishing, gratis, the Dynevor Estate waters where the rule was 'fly only', are very resourceful and worthy of closer study.

This pattern, tied in tube and long-shank versions with 'flying trebles' built into the head, is recommended by Raymond Harris from Oxford - a keen, experienced and expert night fisher on Llangadog waters. He believes that a treble at the head can solve the nip-and-away phenomenon quite effectively.

Bomber

PLATE 1

Hook: 6 or 8 Long shank
Tying silk: Brown
Tail: Deer hair or calf's tail
Body: Clipped deer hair to cigar shape
Rib: Brown or red hackle

This pattern came originally from America where it was used as a salmon fly. Here it has been used mainly as a surface lure for sewin on rivers like the Conway. It is cast across the river and allowed to swing around in its own time without inducing the retrieve. Being made of deer hair, it floats well and can be swung on the surface across the pools and glides. It is effective in fishing for sewin that have been in the river quite a long time, fish, which, for some reason, will ignore the traditional wet fly cast across their path but will come up to hit the Bomber patrolling across the surface.

Brown and Yellow Mole

PLATE 1

Hook: 4 & 5
Tying silk: Black
Tag: Yellow wool
Rib: Gold wire

Body: Rear 1/3, yellow. Front 2/3 mole
Hackle: Ginger
Wing: Brown hen or turkey

A very sober pattern, from one of the most colourful flydressers of the river Towy. Wil Harry's aim with this fly, in all probability, was a pattern calculated to take fish from his favourite runs on the river Towy when the water was down to summer level and success was only to be achieved by subtle but, at the same time, unconventional means. The dark bulky body with the yellow rear and tag being dressed to persuade playful and indifferent fish to go for the business-end of the shank rather than tweak the head - as they will do time after time on summer nights. In recent times, the addition of a small treble with a bright yellow tag attempts the same objective.

It is worth noting that some of these mid-Towy dressings have an appearance which seems to spell a rough and unfinished approach. This suggests, perhaps, the effect of a wounded or struggling creature. Lazy fish will often go for what they consider 'easy pickings' when oxygen levels are low.

This is not to forget that often these flies were tied on the river bank in difficult light conditions with ready-to-hand materials - a heron feather, a bit of sheeps' wool and part of the dressing off an old fly. The light dressing suited rivers like the Towy which normally run clear and shallow in mid-summer which is the height of the sewin season.

Closs Special

PLATE 1

Hook: 8 & 10
Tying silk: Black
Tail: Golden pheasant tippets
Body: Rear half: white tinsel. Front: gold tinsel
Hackle: Orange

Wing: Bronze mallard

Norman Closs-Parry, an angler of considerable all-round ability, devised this fly for use on the river Elwy in Clwyd. Norman is an angler who sometimes adds a maggot to the fly, which helps him to take sewin. This practice is prohibited on the rivers of south and west Wales while it is practised legally and extensively on the rivers of North Wales. It is difficult to quantify how much the fly accounts for the success of the effort and how much the maggot. Some flies do seem to work better with the maggot than do others, and this, apparently, is one of them.

Some sewin anglers on North Wales rivers who would never dream of fishing for sewin without a maggot on the fly, believe fervently in the creed that a maggot converts all the nips and pulls felt on 'fly only' tackle into firm pulls. This is not always so and, even with the use of maggots, sewin will often just 'tweak' the maggot - much as a trout will do with a worm. The use of a flying, small-size fourteen double or treble hook is then advised.

Conway Badger

PLATE 1

Hook: 6 & 8
Tying silk: Black
Rib: Three turns of flat red tinsel
Body: Black floss
Wing: Twelve hairs from badger back

This old pattern, originating from the river Conway, is very similar to the Conway Red which is more widely used today. The three turns of red tinsel make for a predominantly black body and this is the tellingly attractive feature of the pattern according to Roy Jones, the Head Keeper on the Gwydir Hotel water on the river Conway. Roy also is adamant about the number of hairs used to make the wing. The number twelve is both puzzling and surprising. It allows for the body to be clearly visible - veiled, as it were, by the few hairs which are more active and attractive for their sparseness. Roy also maintains that the correct procedure in tying the wing is important. The hair is tied out over the eye and then folded back and tied again so that it rests back over the body. This makes for a rather more bulky head, which is believed to give the fly the required action in the water. The fly has no hackle: and is somewhat unusual in this respect. The folding-over of the wing ensures that there is no danger of the hairs being lost, as sometimes happens with poorly tied flies.

Conway Red

PLATE 1

Hook: 6 & 8
Tying silk: Black
Rib: Thin flat red tinsel
Body: Black floss
Wing: Hairs from badger back

This is a more common version of the Conway Badger without the meticulous restrictions on materials. This variant has travelled well and finds favour with anglers in other parts of the Principality. During warm weather when the sewin tend to be in the more quick-flowing parts of the river, the Conway Red, fished on a floating line, does very well. It is a far more bulky creation than the Conway Badger, making more disturbance when fished in the surface film - thereby attracting more attention to itself.

Cooke's Bogey

PLATE 1

Head: 8 & 9
Tying silk: Black
Tag: Silver tinsel

Body: Black ostrich herl
Rib: Silver thread
Wing: White hen secondary quill
Hackle: Badger cock

Pryce Tannatt produced some excellent fly patterns which are masterpieces of the art of flydressing. This pattern has achieved considerable success as a late evening sedge and also as a sewin fly. When used in the late evening, it is advisable to use a floating line to 'skit' the fly across the surface of the water. Often the fly will be ignored completely until the angler begins to move it. It has the added advantage of being highly visible as darkness approaches.

In its role as a sewin fly, many anglers find it successful for the first hour after darkness when fished on a floating line. The aim then is to have it fishing just under the surface and a short, sink-tip or, better still, slow-sink line does this job rather well.

It is a pity that this pattern is not better known and more widely used - as it certainly can be great help. Yet is is often the case that one particular angler can stumble across a pattern which will work well for him but always disappoint the next man. On the river Taf at Saint Clears the fishing for sewin at night can be exceptionally good where sewin of up to twenty pounds are seen every year. Cooke's Bogey is a pattern for the smaller sewin which move upriver after the big sewin have moved on to the higher reaches. These smaller sewin provide good sport though there are arguments for not making serious depredations of them. Bag limits of two or three brace should be observed by responsible anglers. It often pays to move the fly rather quickly as these smaller sewin are extremely active and playful and will chase anything fished near the surface. Unfortunately this active period is all too short and the angler must be ready to react quickly at such times.

Dai Ben

PLATE 2

Hook: 6, 8 & 10
Tying silk: Black
Tail: Honey dun fibres
Rib: Flat silver tinsel
Body: Rabbit fur
Hackle: Honey dun

This fly reigned supreme in the fifties and sixties on the river Towy where it took over from and displaced the Silver Invicta and Teal, Black & Silver. Today it is not so widely used. It was a fly designed for day as well as night fishing and did well on the tidal reaches - especially as the tide ran out.

It was baptised by David Benjamin Glyn Davies, a great fly fisherman from Abergwili, near Carmarthen, on the river Towy. He maintains he received the pattern from Lord Dynevor's coachman. As Mr Davies did not tie his own flies he sent the pattern off to the Cummings Fishing Tackle firm and ordered a couple of dozen. For reference purposes he was asked to name it; he used his own first names, 'Dai' being short for David and 'Ben' for Benjamin.

As the season progresses, a darker hackle is preferable. The fly is tied rather full with plenty of guard fibres sticking out to give the whole fly an animated effect when drawn through the water. The rabbit fur to be used is best taken from the back of a rabbit, taking only the top layer of fur.

When the normal three-fly cast for sewin is used, the Dai Ben should generally go on the point. The modern tendency is to use a two-fly cast with just the one dropper which invariably is a fly of a smaller size. Dai Ben has the reputation of being a good day-time fly particularly on a river like the Towy which is controlled by a reservoir in its upper reaches. These rivers, of which there are many in Wales, often have high water without much colour. Under such conditions the Dai Ben fishes well.

This is basically a Towy pattern and it must be accepted that it does not work well on many other rivers. Prolonged trials have revealed that it does not meet with much success on the rivers Teifi, Taf, Dovey or Conway while it has accounted for some fish on the Dwyfawr, Dwyryd, Rheidiol and Cleddau.

Probably the most surprising success achieved by the Dai Ben has been on the Towy Estuary. Some anglers do rather well by fishing the tail of the tide. This is quite good fishing and the Dai Ben seems to be the kind of pattern to offer to the sewin that hang back in the pools as the tide drains away.

Doctor's Special

PLATE 2

Hook: 9 or 12
Tying silk: Brown
Tail: Ginger cock strands
Rib: Fine gold wire
Body: Fawn or cinnamon fur from base of hare's ear
Hackle: Coch-a-bon-ddu
Wing: Bronze mallard

Dr Shelton Roberts, who fished many of the Lleyn rivers in North Wales, favoured drab-coloured flies in his approach to sewin fishing. Fifty years ago the fancy coloured flies - with their sparkling tinsel - were not as popular as they are today; and flies were generally far smaller. The doctor used a size nine hook for high water conditions and a size twelve hook for very low water conditions.

When fishing the Dwyfach, a very small river, in low water conditions the wet-fly cast used was often no longer than four feet - yet it supported two or three wet flies which were no more than nine to twelve inches apart!

Dovey Black & Orange

PLATE 2

Hook: 4,6 or 8, or size 6 salmon double
Tying silk: Black
Tail: Red swan
Rib: Silver thread
Body: Black floss
Hackle: Orange
Wing: Black squirrel
Cheeks: Jungle cock

Another excellent pattern from one of the premier sewin rivers in Wales. Most examples are tied on number six doubles which give the pattern extra hooking capability.

This pattern has the advantage of being an excellent taker of sewin irrespective of the level of water in which it is being fished. As on most rivers, the Dovey sewin give anglers a couple of hours of near-surface activity before midnight when the Black & Orange serves well. Fished then on a floating or a short sink-tip line the fly provides good colour and visibility in all conditions.

The Dovey Black & Orange has been successful on the Glaslyn, Dwyfawr and Conway. Sewin anglers today look for good colour contrast in their sewin flies and the drab, sober colours of years gone by are tending to give way to more vivid combinations. Emyr Lloyd, a river keeper on the Dovey, recommends this pattern and believes that it is a must on the Dovey.

Dovey Bumble

PLATE 2

Hook: 6, 8 &10
Tying silk: Black
Rib: Silver thread
Tag: Silver thread
Body: Green peacock herl tied full

Hackle: Barred Plymouth Rock

The river Dovey, one of the most prolific sewin rivers in the Principality, has its own special Bumble pattern. It bears little resemblance to the Bumble series from Derbyshire.

The Dovey Bumble is tied with two hackles; the smaller of the two being used to palmer the body down. Some dressers, in the interest of better hooking, add a small amount of hackle down along the body. The river Dovey is normally a clear river when not in flood, and the Dovey Bumble looks well when fished in the runs. At night this pattern can be used as a dropper with a bigger point fly. In recent years some anglers have been using the Dovey Bumble in a tandem form.

During the thirties many different Bumble patterns were tried on the Dovey for sewin. It would appear that none of the variations (listed below) have been as successful as this one.

Yellow Bumble

PLATE 2

Hook: 6, 8, & 10
Tying silk: Yellow
Tail: Golden pheasant toppings
Rib: Gold thread
Body: Golden olive seal's fur
Hackle: Yellow (palmered)
Front Hackle: Blue jay

This pattern has gained much favour with anglers fishing in water which is clearing after a flood.

Fiery Brown Bumble

PLATE 2

Hook: 6-10
Tying silk: Brown
Tail: Golden pheasant toppings

Rib: Gold thread
Body: Fiery brown seal's fur
Hackle: Red and fiery brown mixed
Front **hackle:** Grouse hackle

This pattern is used in fast-flowing water when the river level is down to low summer flow.

Claret Bumble

PLATE 2

Hook: 6-10
Tying silk: Claret
Tail: Golden pheasant tippets
Rib: Gold thread
Body: Claret seal's fur
Hackle: Claret and black hackles mixed
Front **hackle:** Jay

The Claret Bumble is used mostly at dusk and is fished on the bob position when moths are hovering near the water.

Earley's Fancy (No 1)

PLATE 2

Hook: No 10 or 11 (Salmon size)
Tying silk: Brown
Tail: Toppings
Rib: Gold twist
Body: Rusty re-brown fur
Hackle: Same colour (or lighter) than body
Wing: Cock pheasant

See Earley's Fancy (No 2)

Earley's Fancy (No 2)

PLATE 2

Hook: 10 or 11 (Two sizes smaller than for number 1)
Tying silk: Brown
Tail: A few springs of tippets
Rib: Gold tinsel
Body: Dark claret fur

Hackle: Coch-a-bon-ddu stained claret
Wing: Cock pheasant

Francis Francis in his *A Book of Angling*, published in 1867, notes some popular 'sewin flies' which he received from 'a Mr Berrington' who was a respected angler on the rivers Ogmore and Ewenny. Those rivers then enjoyed the reputation of being excellent sewin rivers; some anglers even considering them to be the best in Wales. George Agar Hansard who, in 1834, listed some of the catches made on the Ogmore, was one who maintained that it was without equal as a sewin river. Ominously though, there were already some problems in respect of pollution.

These two Earley's Fancy flies were used for sewin in low and high water and were useful as salmon flies as well.

Evening Serenade

PLATE 5

Hook: 8 & 10
Tying silk: Black
Body: Black wool, black seal's fur or flat silver
Rib: Silver thread
Hackle: Blue cock
Front hackle: Teal or grey partridge
Cheeks: Jungle cock (optional)

The dressing here is rather bushy, much in the manner of bob flies. Many anglers use two blue hackles and then wind the teal or partridge hackle through the blue hackle. The tag is added as it is often used during the day on the dropper of a two-fly leader. The red fluorescent tag adds to its allure when used on rivers as a surface, skating fly.

The addition of Jungle Cock is a must for some anglers but this is a personal whim. As this is primarily a fly for stillwaters the cheeks are not so important. On lakes like Talyllyn and Coron it will also take brown trout. Evening Serenade is considered to do rather well on the white trout in Ireland at dusk, hence its name.

Fiery Brown

PLATE 3

Hook: 8 or 10
Tying silk: Brown
Tail: Golden pheasant tail
Rib: Gold wire
Body: Brown
Wing: Bronze mallard

The Fiery Brown is a comparatively little-known sewin fly, despite the fact that it was voted as the best seatrout fly in Ireland in 1905, where, in an Exhibition of Fishing, by inviting each area to nominate their favourite fly, it swept the board. It is still a good general pattern to use for sewin fishing during the day, especially with stale fish.

Much of the sewin fishing done in Wales is on angling club or association water and the approach, therefore, has to be different to that for fishing private, undisturbed water. Some anglers may, on occasion, have to share a pool with as many as eight or ten other rods - and many of those will be using different baits and methods. Under such circumstances the angler is well advised to modify his approach and consider flies of smaller dimensions and more refined colours. The Fiery Brown fits this bill admirably and it is a good fly for taking shy sewin. Fished on a floating line and worked slowly down and around the pool at dusk it will take the odd reluctant sewin by surprise.

In size ten, used during daylight hours, the Fiery Brown, despite its Irish origin, has the appearance of a typical Welsh fly for sewin. Fished then in the runs and the necks of pools it will take sewin in the early hours of the morning.

Fiery Jack

PLATE 5

Hook: 8 or 10 single and on a Waddington iron
Tying silk: Black
Body: Dark red seal's fur
Rib: Flat red tinsel
Hackle: Scarlet cock
Wing: Brown mallard or red squirrel

The style of dressing Fiery Jack is that of the normal wet-fly with some two or three turns of good scarlet hackle. The wing of either red squirrel or brown mallard is dressed long and at an angle of some forty-five degrees.

It is an excellent fly in the late evening and in the first hour of darkness. Many anglers prefer this to the more popular and widely-known Red or Dark Mackerel. It is generally used on a two fly leader. Some notable anglers use it as a dropper and find that the smaller version will take sewin when fished during daylight under windy conditions.

A visiting angler from Manchester made this pattern his favourite and it has an enviable record on the middle stretches of the Mawddach. He fishes it on a small Waddington iron and favours a treble with barbs on the outside of the hook. These comparatively newly-designed trebles are now on the sewin scene and no doubt will be subjected to increasing tests in the coming seasons.

Some anglers use a pattern known as Water Rat & Red by Dr Shelton Roberts in a team with Fiery Jack. Some flies appear to work well as a team, as do the above pair.

Grey Goose (Llwyd yr Wydd)

PLATE 3

Hook: 7, 9 & 12
Tying silk: Brown
Tail: 3 or 4 strands of mallard
Body: Hare's ear (dark)
Rib: Silver tinsel
Hackle: Dark red cock
Wing: Saddle feather from goose

This is one of a series of flies that Dr Shelton Roberts, a GP in Penygroes, near Caernarvon in North Wales, used some fifty years ago.

Dr Shelton Roberts was of the opinion that Llwyd yr Wydd was the very best sewin fly for the rivers Dwyfawr and Dwyfach. These rivers today hold some very big sewin, up to ten pounds and more in weight, which normally respond better to big lures. Smaller flies like the Llwyd yr Wydd can often rouse them though, when they are bored with being shown big tubes and Terrors.

Harry Tom

PLATE 3

Hook: 8 &10
Tying silk: Brown
Tail: Honey dun fibres
Rib: Silver wire
Body: Rabbit fur
Hackle: Honey dun
Wing: Bronze mallard

The Harry Tom fly, from the Ogwen valley in North Wales, is somewhat similar to the Dai Ben from the Towy Valley, in south-west Wales. The rabbit fur used in both patterns must be from the top layer of a rabbit's back.

As with many sewin flies, this pattern is drab in appearances and suitable for both day and night fishing. In North Wales it is customary to impale a maggot onto the fly hook - a practice deemed to improve its attractiveness (though it is debatable if it is then true flyfishing) - and the Harry Tom seems to work well with a maggot.

The tendency today is to use bigger, silver bodied lures for night fishing and many of the traditional patterns like the Harry Tom tend now to be used as droppers. Still used on the river of North Wales.

Huw Nain

PLATE 3

Hook: 6 & 8
Tying silk: Brown
Tail: Tippets
Rib: Silver wire
Body: Rear half: golden olive. Front half: grey seal's fur
Wing: Hen pheasant
Hackle: Partridge

A good fly from the Dolwyddelan area. Dressed by Eirwyn Roberts, it pleases anglers on the Conway and its tributaries very well. This pattern has a long tradition in North Wales, being popular also on the Dwyryd and Dyfawr. It is used both during the day and at night and has the reputation of being very successful in the taking of big sewin.

The name 'Huw Nain' suggests that a certain Huw (the Welsh spelling of Hugh) was involved in the creation of this pattern. The word 'Nain' means Grandmother in Welsh, which is interesting - as it dates the pattern to an earlier era when boys with over-common names acquired nicknames. It sounds as if in his youth this fisherman was reared by his grandmother.

The fly works well on other rivers in Wales when fished in quick runs during the daytime. In the early days of sewin fishing the all-through-the-night sessions were not so common. Many of the ordinary workmen

in North Wales in those days had very little time to fish. They often worked a twelve hour day. They would go out at dusk and fish until midnight, and their flies were designed to take the smaller sewin. The big sewin that are generally the post-midnight takers did not figure prominently in the workmen's bags. Yet Huw Nain achieved the reputation of being good at taking big sewin - which points something of a contradiction.

Those anglers who fish for rainbow trout can do much worse than try Huw Nain on them; it has been known to do well on Eglwys Nunydd Reservoir at Port Talbot.

Kingsmill

PLATE 3

Hook: 6 & 8
Tying silk: Black
Tail: Golden pheasant topping
Tag: Blue floss tied broad and prominent
Rib: Silver wire
Body: Black ostrich herl
Hackle: Black cock
Wing: Rook secondary rolled and tied low
Cheeks: Jungle cock
Topping: As roof over all golden pheasant topping

The Kingsmill invented by T.C. Kingsmill Moore for use in the Irish Loughs in the 1950s is a good point fly on a three-fly cast fished downstream on rivers such as the Teifi and Rheidol. It works best used on a floating line or a sink tip. The fly should be kept in the surface layer of the water and is effective when it swings round - fishing 'round the bend'. It works well when the sewin have been in the river for some time. The dressing should be very light and the body rather thick.

It is a stalwart during the hours of darkness but it is also useful during the day and is even known to take a few salmon at the tail end of the season.

Lewi's Killer

PLATE 3

Hook: 6
Tying silk: Black
Tail: Black fibres
Body: Black wool
Rib: two distinct bands of gold thread
Hackle: Long black hen drawn below the body

Today the Black Lure is the top reservoir lure. It is interesting that Lewi Davies of Llandeilo devised this pattern sometime in the thirties. The success gained by black fly patterns for stillwater trout is well known in all part of Wales, but it was thought that the Black Lure has only become widely used in sewin fishing after the evidence of its success in reservoir fishing.

Few Welsh anglers between the wars would ever have thought of using a black lure for night sewin fishing, but Lewi Davies did and had success with it. The Black Lure is always fished deep and slow and has the deserved reputation of taking big fish. It is best fished in high water - and can attract salmon too.

That the Black Lure was being used on the river Towy in the thirties in a manner identical to the latest reservoir approach is very intriguing. Why did Lewi in those early days employ only an apron of hackle as opposed to the normal method of winding the hackle around the hook? It is said that some of the old Welsh flydressers working in isolation were really gifted, and that some of them lived out of their time.

Lewi's Killer had a gold band around the middle, another unusual feature of his bold approach to flydressing. Could this have been an attempt at getting the sewin to hit the centre of the lure as opposed to tweaking its head or bottom? This principle of attaching a band of (fluorescent) material around the centre of the body material - was tried a few years ago, and it was thought then to be an innovation.

Lewi did not always give his flies names. He gave examples of his successes to particular friends and when asked what it was, he would blink and nudge, 'Never mind, take it, use it. It's a killer, mind!' So we named this after the inventor, 'Lewi's Killer'.

Mallard & Silver

PLATE 3

Hook: 8 & 10
Tying silk: Black
Tail: Golden pheasant tippets
Rib: Silver wire
Body: Flat silver tinsel
Hackle: Black hen
Wing: Bronze mallard

This fly was very popular in the fifties and sixties and was a great favourite with Peter Vaughan, the well-known fishing tackle dealer at Machynlleth, who recommended an alternative double-hook tying where conditions demanded a rapid and deeper-sinking attractor.

In those days the three-wet-fly team fished down-river was the normal method of fishing for sewin. One angler who, according to his diaries, fished the Dovey at that time some four nights every week, invariably used the same three-fly cast combination throughout the sewin season. His point fly was the Haslam; his bob fly always the Dovey Bumble. In the early years he had used various flies in the middle dropper position until Peter Vaughan persuaded him to try the Silver Mallard. He never changed the dramatis personae of his cast thereafter.

Marchog Coch *(Red Knight)*

PLATE 3

Hook: 8 & 10
Tying silk: Red
Butt: Red silk
Body: Flat gold tinsel ribbed with fine silver wire
Wing: Paired red tail feathers from golden pheasant
Outer: Yellow body feathers from golden pheasant
Topping: four strands of peacock sword

To make the flying treble mount:
Three strands of 20lb black nylon looped around treble, then plaited. Attach plaited nylon to shank of main hook - whip firmly and trim

A colourful sewin pattern which has many excellent qualities. The stiff tail feathers of the golden pheasant ride well in the water and will not wrap around the hooks - as is the tendency with softer hackle fibres.

The flying treble, some two or three inches behind the hook, is made of black plaited 20lb nylon which is an excellent link. The weight of the fly can be increased or decreased by judicious use of heavier and lighter hooks. If the angler, wishes to gain maximum depth, the use of a double hook for the body is recommended.

This lure is the brainchild of Dr Graeme Harris of the Welsh Water Authority, who does much of his fishing on the river Dovey. The Marchog series is primarily designed to take the big sewin for which the river Dovey is rightly famed.

Marchog Glas *(Blue Knight)*

PLATE 3

Hook: 8 & 10
Tying silk: Black
Butt: Red fluorescent wool

Body: Silver tinsel ribbed with gold
Hackle: Golden pheasant red body hackle
Wing: Two pairs of blue feathers
Cheeks: A Plymouth Rock feather
Topping: Four strands of peacock herl

The Marchog Glas is similar to its brother the Red Knight and also has a reputation for taking really big fish. When the sewin become dour, the Marchog Glas fished on a quick-sinking line is really effective. The flying treble - especially when of the out point variety - is an excellent hooker. Often, sewin anglers lose these big sewin when only lightly hooked. Trebles can help to eliminate this problem.

The Marchog series, soundly based as they are in the traditional mainstream of sewin attractors, are very much flies of the late twentieth century - for sewin and for stillwater trout.

Moc's Beauty

PLATE 5

Hook: 6 or 8 or one inch Waddington iron
Tying silk: Black
Body: Rear half: Flat gold tinsel. Front half: red seal's fur
Ribbing: Gold wire
Hackle: Black hen
Wing: Yellow & squirrel hair
Cheeks: Jungle cock (optional)

This fly is dressed portly with a full wing and heavy hackle. The seal fur dressed tight under the wing gives the fly good movement when pulled against the water. The tricolour-wing of black, orange and yellow has a good record for autumn-running sewin.

This fly has its origins in the fly patterns used by George Agar Hansard in 1834 to fish for trout in the Teifi. At that time it was used mainly during the day and there is very little information about sewin fishing in those days.

The colourful feathers used for the original fly are something of a surprise as the salmon flies used by Hansard were usually sombre efforts. Yellow was an important colour and many salmon patterns used in angling on the Wye and the Usk in those days had a lot of yellow wool in them. Most of those patterns, especially those used by the Hext Lewis family in their beats on the Upper Wye, came in a dirty yellow, the Welsh term being 'Melyn Budr'.

The modern version has a good colour pattern and has an impressive catching record. The best position for it is as a dropper and its lightish hew makes it a very effective fly to fish the upper layers of the water.

Moc's Bumble

PLATE 5

Hook: 6 & 8
Tying silk: Black
Body: Flat Silver
Hackle: Blue cock
Wing: Blue Calf Tail or blue squirrel tail
HEAD: Muddler - deer hair

The muddler head is to be dressed rather sparsely and clipped tightly. A few strands of blue lureflash adds to the effectiveness of the wing.

The bumble is used mainly as a bob fly on a two fly leader. When casting across-river the Bumble will keep near the surface and float in the surface film if the rod is held upright; an ideal dropper, as it causes a buzz in the upper layers of the water.

It has proved very effective on moonlit nights when sewin tend to be very wary. On such occasions anglers can use Moc's Bumble much as they would a dry fly, letting it drift down naturally with the current.

Moc's Cert

PLATE 5

Hook: 6 or 8 single. One to two inches long Waddington
Tying silk: Black
Body: Rear half - silver tinsel; Front half - black seal's fur
Hackle: Black hen
Wing: Black squirrel
Over Wing: Peacock sword feathers with green lureflash (optional)
Cheeks: Jungle cock

This fly, dressed heavily with a prominent thorax, is best used as a point fly. It was designed by a committee of four mad sewin anglers with immense sewin experience who were asked to devise a fly which had, in their opinion, the main trigger-points of a good sewin fly. It was considered, in order to get the best of both worlds, to have a body half silver and half black seal's fur. The silver section gives the glint and the black seal's fur gives a very attractive iridescent colour pattern. In recent seasons a few strands of luminous green lureflash have been added to the wing.

The Jungle Cock cheeks add the all important colour factor of the completed fly. Many serious sewin anglers add Jungle Cock cheeks to all their sewin flies. Members of the ad hoc committee argued fiercely about the form and shape of the fly and while one favoured a sleek slim line so common with many other sewin flies, the others preferred the pattern to have that all-important 'buzz' which adds to the attractiveness of the fly - giving it life and a presence.

The name given to the fly is misleading - no fly is a Cert yet it is a tribute to the effectiveness of the pattern that has taken a lot of fish under very difficult conditions.

Midnight Magic

PLATE 5

Hook: 8 Single or Double
Tying silk: Black
Tag: Green fluorescent wool
Rib: Silver wire
Body: Black wool or flat silver tinsel
Body hackle: Black cock (palmered)
Front hackle: Small teal or grey partridge

This fly is dressed bushily with plenty of hackle tied palmered style. The teal hackle is often wound right through the black hackle and this results in a very attractive colour pattern. Many anglers use a grey partridge feather instead of a teal.

This fly is good at getting sewin to move to it - although at times it is a poor hooker. Sewin will often seem to nudge it. On rivers, as the water is thinning after a flood, it does well when fished in the surface of the water. Generally sewin anglers use a two-fly leader with Midnight Magic on the bob just under the surface where it causes quite a buzz. Some of the Cardiff stable of sewin anglers on the upper Towy swear by the buzz of the fly and some even use as many as four hackles on the fly, very much in the 'Loch Ordie' style.

I recall one angler on the river Dwyfor casting Midnight Magic across those fish-holding pools which have been so brilliantly constructed by the Llanystumdwy anglers, and just letting it drift across the surface. It effectively attracted the sewin up from the deeps to take it and on such occasions it really does demonstrate the magic element in its name.

Mouse (or Surface Lure)

PLATE 4

Hook: 6 with flying treble.
Tying silk: White
Body: White deer hair clipped
Wing: Deer hair and marabou

The mouse is a surface lure whose purpose is to create a wake by skating across the surface of the water. The wake is the attraction more than the fly itself. Years ago, sewin angers used a huge cork-based version of this lure constructed from half a wine-cork cut lengthways and shaped, with a 4/0 salmon hook protruding - eye-uppermost - through the cork, which was adorned with bushy, colourful feathers. The Mouse was cast onto the surface of the water and allowed to drift around. So effective was it on some rivers that it was actually banned.

Not all pools are suited to this method of fishing: it is essential that there is a firm flow to enable the lure to be swung around and across the river. A long rod allows for greater control of the lure. The Mouse will sometimes take sewin, fishing in a semi-submerged state, in the manner of the bob fly.

There is no doubt that there is a period during most warm nights when it is worth trying the surface lure. Even if it fails to hook, it has the distinct advantage of showing the angler where the sewin are holding up because it often moves fish which otherwise do not show. One very successful angler on the river Towy does not use any other lure for his sewin fishing and his results are impressive - especially with big fish.

While the surface lure is designed to skate across the surface, it is possible to use this same lure in another way. This demands that the lure sink just a few inches below the surface - and is then stripped quickly, really quickly, across the pool. This tactic is best used with a short, sink-tip or an intermediate line. The surface lure is one of the most neglected devices in sewin fishing and, whether drifted across the river, or stripped quickly in, or fished just under the surface, it represents a most exciting method.

Some anglers also recommend holding the surface lure in a run and moving it slowly by carefully raising the rod: this is known as 'dibbing' or 'dibbling', which can also do the trick in bringing up very good fish. Needless to add, with such tactics, very many fish are missed: yet on some nights every one will be fast on the flying treble.

Night Heron

PLATE 4

Hook: 6
Tying silk: Black
Tag: Silver wire
Body: Black wool, ribbed with silver
Front half: Black silk, varnished
Hackle: Mid body, heron

This fly, devised by Lewi Davies of Llandeilo, was a complete innovation in the late forties when it was first used. He must have decided to attach the hackle mid-way down the body in order to try and combat the tendency to nip the fly which can be so infuriating when fish are somewhat stale and in shoals in low water conditions, and at other times when this unaccountable behaviour is observable. Lewi, though not the world's neatest flydresser, was remarkably scientific in his approach.

Today we think of the Dog Nobbler as the newest reservoir lure which has adopted the same principle. The modern material used with such flies is marabou feather with its long fluffy fibres, but Lewi Davies, by utilising the soft heron feathers, had achieved the same effect by 1950.

The heron herl used by Lewi as centre hackle for this pattern is ideal material for this sewin fly. Modern flydressers use marabou for the same purpose, but it is doubtful if it is as effective. Most sewin anglers in the days of Lewi Davies retrieved their flies by the simple figure-of-eight action of the hand. This works the flies in a slow, jerky action which activates the long hackle.

Old Favourite

PLATE 4

Hook: 9 & 12
Tying silk: Claret
Rib: Yellow silk thread
Body: Wine-coloured wool and dark hare's ear
Hackle: Partridge

This fly was described by Dr Shelton Roberts, who fished the Lleyn, as his favourite sewin fly. As in most of his patterns, the hook sizes are numbers nine and twelve: somewhat unusual. The Doctor's patterns form a valuable contribution to flydressing in North Wales.

This pattern closely resembles the Tom Tom from the Cwmystwyth area of mid-Wales, the identical body being used as a wet fly when the alder is on the water; though the hackle used by Thomas Thomas for the Tom Tom varied from partridge to grouse. It seems that the Tom Tom sported the partridge hackle early in the season and the darker grouse hackle later on.

Polly Perkins

PLATE 2

Hook: 12 (salmon size)
Tying silk: Brown
Tag: Gold twist
Tail: Sprigs of tippet
Body: Peacock herl
Rib: Fine gold wire
Hackle: Coch-a-bon-ddu
Wing: Two small tippet feathers
Cheek: Small kingfishers
Ribs: Blue macaw

A fly first mentioned by Francis Francis, in

his *Book of Angling* (1867) presumably recalling the popular Music Hall song of the day:

> She was as beautiful as a butterfly,
> And as proud as a Queen
> Was pretty little Polly Perkins
> of Paddington Green

Princess Di

PLATE 5

Hook: 6 or 8
Tying silk: Black
Body: Yellow seal's fur
Rib: Flat gold tinsel
Hackle: Blue (kingfisher)
Wing: Grey squirrel with white marabou overwing
Cheeks: Jungle cock

This is a colourful pattern and is certainly a good looker. The body should be bright yellow, with a bold gold ribbing. Some anglers dress it with a white-and-grey wing while some put on a multi-colour wing of orange, yellow and black. The fly has a slim-line form and many anglers add the jungle cock cheeks.

The body and hackle bear similarity with flies used in the nineteenth century especially on the Wye and I was informed of a display board of similar coloured flies in a certain museum. Unfortunately on my second visit when I had more time to study the display I discovered that the display panel of flies had disappeared from the museum. Subsequent visits to the museum were equally unsuccessful. Pity, this, as much of the history of fishing in certain localities in Wales has been lost.

Many night anglers use Princess Di as a dropper and for some unknown reason swear that the fly works best on cold nights. There is no doubt that it works well on the bob when used in a two fly team with a dark fly like the Cert or Snowdrop on the point - the

contrast being very effective.

The addition of the white marabou is something of a modern appendix but for some reason it has a good record on moonlit nights. The version with a darker wing has also found favour with fishers on high and coloured water.

Yellow bodied flies are now becoming popular again 'à la' Cat's Whiskers after quite a long spell of being out of favour.

Pry-copyn

PLATE 4

Hook: 6, 8 & 10
Tying silk: Black
Tag: Red ibis or red wool
Rib: Thin silver wire
Body: Grey seal's fur
Hackle: Well-marked badger

This is an old Welsh pattern which was used for sewin fishing on the rivers Glaslyn and Dwyryd with considerable success. It is not so widely used to day, except by a few of the older generation of sewin anglers. Some find it especially effective when used with a maggot, a method which is illegal in south and west Wales.

The badger hackle has been a favourite in Wales on many rivers and for many years. The tendency is to use it in hot, bright conditions. It is a highly visible feather which accounts for its being used when the river is just losing its colour after a flood. Some anglers also use the Pry-copyn in smaller sizes for day-time sewin fishing when the water is low.

Sewin can be taken during the day, but the angler is well advised to disguise his approach and it is necessary to work up-river. There is also an advantage in adding a little weight to the dressing so that the fly, when fished up-river, sinks immediately and can be drifted at the level at which the sewin are lying.

Remember that it is most necessary to sink the fly down to that eye-ball to eye-ball level when fishing for sewin during the day. They will seldom rise and take a fly on the surface like trout.

Pussy Galore

PLATE 5

Hook: 8 or 10
Tying silk: White
Tail: White marabou
body: Yellow floss or yellow seal's fur
Rib: Silver or gold thread
Wing: White marabou
Head: Gold bead

Sewin fishing was probably the last of the games fishing disciplines to use goldheads. Pussy Galore with its yellow body and white wing is an exceptionally colourful sewin fly. It has an enticing action when pulled across the current in a sink and draw action. The Goldhead had proved a boon for all anglers as it has enabled them to fish deep at certain times and the goldhead is effective in sinking the fly right to the bed of the river.

This is one fly pattern whose full value is yet to be realised.

Sewin fishing during daylight has developed much in the last decade especially on the Dyfi and Tywi and with refined leader and a Pussy Galore, the angler can fish very deep amongst the sewin which generally hug the river bed on bright days.

Very few anglers have really mastered the classical method of fishing a nymph for sewin. It can be very effective when the angler is fishing up-river and bumps the goldhead along the bottom. The angler is well-advised to concentrate on one specific fish and not attack the leading fish in the shoal even though, more often than not, that will be the best fish in the pool.

Rancid Racoon

PLATE 4

Hook: 6 or 8
Tying silk: Black
Tail: Golden pheasant toppings
Body: Gold lurex
Rib: Gold wire
Hackle: Black cock (palmered)
Throat hackle: Natural gallina
Wing: Grey squirrel
Cheeks: Jungle cock

This fly was devised by Winston Oliver, known as 'Scruff Oliver', who fishes the Red House beats on the Eastern Cleddau in Pembrokeshire. It was designed as a night fly, but it has proved successful during the day as well. it is tied generally on a number six hook with the squirrel tail extending out beyond the bend about half the length of the iron. The whole tying should be done with the maximum economy of materials.

When required to fish low in the water it is tied on a number ten double salmon hook. In this guise Rancid Racoon has also accounted for a number of salmon on the Eastern Cleddau.

Red Mackerel

PLATE 4

Hook: 6 & 8
Tying silk: Red
Tail: Bronze mallard
Body: Red lurex
Hackle: Blood red hackle
Wing: Bronze mallard

This fly originated in North Wales, but its fame spread quickly to other parts of the Principality. In this expansion of its territory, the pattern suffered a debasement of its original dressing. In some areas patterns masquerading under the title Red Mackerel bear little or no resemblance to the authentic dressing given above.

Of bigger sewin rivers like the Dovey and the Towy, the Red Mackerel does quite well when the river is running down and losing its colour. The modern tendency in such conditions is for anglers to resort to the use of spinning equipment. Use of the colourful Red Mackerel can be equally effective, particularly in taking stale fish that have been in the river for some time and are wise to the ironmongery that is hurled at them.

On the river Cleddau, when the main run of smaller sewin comes in during late July, I know of one particular angler who does well with the Red Mackerel.

Silver Grey

PLATE 4

Hook: 6 & 8
Tying silk: Black
Tail: Golden pheasant tippets
Body: Silver tinsel
Rib: Silver wire
Hackle: Badger hackle
Wing: Teal

The Conway is considered one of the finest sewin rivers in Wales. A sewin angler of repute in the sixties was J.O. Jones. The Silver Grey was his brainchild and, while there were many who tied the pattern, few scored the same success with it as 'J.O.' He tied his flies very lightly and the teal flank feather was tied very short, often not reaching back more than to half the hook. This Conway sewin fly is not to be confused with the classic salmon pattern.

Some anglers used to use pigeon feather instead of the teal flank feather - because of its better marking and closer webb. The tendency today is to use grey squirrel as wing.

Teifi Terror

PLATE 4

Hook: 10 & 8
Tying silk: Black
Rib: Gold wire
Tail: Furnace fibres
Body: Black floss
Hackle: Furnace

The Teifi Terror, once a traditional sewin fly, is more often than not these days tied as a tandem. This enables the angler to present to the fish a bigger lure, one with added hooking potential.

In its original form, tied solo on size 10 or 8 hook, in the middle reaches of the Teifi, the Teifi Terror is still capable of doing well, fished in the traditional manner with a more gentle approach. It is a fly that can be fished with either a floating or sink-tip line.

The river Teifi is often peat-stained when running down after a flood and it needs a flashy solution to the problem of attracting the fish; the Teifi Terror is then, in daylight, particularly effective.

In its tandem from the Teifi Terror is a late-night or near-dawn lure. Generally, big lures are fished on quick-sinking lines and are stripped along the bottom of the pool. Big sewin often lie close to the river bed and these big lures can sometimes tempt them to take. Tactics like these are worth trying on heavily-fished rivers.

Tom Tom

PLATE 4

Hook: 8
Tying silk: Yellow
Rib: Silver thread
Body: Pig's hair
Hackle: Greenwell
Wing: Bronze mallard

This pattern comes from the box of Thomas

Thomas who lived the latter part of his life in the Cwmystwyth area and before that in Llangurig and in Maentwrog. He was an accomplished flydresser - all his patterns dressed on eye-less hooks. Most were dressed in the North Wales manner - except this particular one. The Tom Tom was liberally hackled in the tradition of the 'shaving brush', over-hackled flies, sometimes known as 'Loch Maree style'.

Pig's hair, although easily available in the days when practically every household kept a pig at the end of the garden, was a material not often used by flydressers. The pig's soft bristle gave the fly a yellowish tinge and this made it highly visible - even in the most dirty water. The pig's hair body also made for a very buoyant fly which is quite active when moved through the water.

It is interesting to note that it was often the custom in Wales to have the same christian and surname, and so Thomas Thomas was invariably known as Tom Tom - just as Morgan Morgan is known as Moc Morgan! (*see* Old Favourite)

T. L. Harries Sedge

PLATE 4

Hook: 8
Tying silk: Brown
Body: Peacock herl
Hackle: Three or four ginger cock hackles
Wing: Partridge hackle

This sedge is dressed very full, with four strands of peacock herl twisted into a rope and put around the iron. Three or four ginger hackles are tied in to form a very bushy hackle. The line and cast were kept off the surface of the water, bringing the fly around to form a big wake. The wake was just as important as the fly itself.

In fishing a pattern like this, the rod is held high and lifted up now and then just as one would with a bob fly. The action of lifting the fly up from the water will often move fish that have been indifferent to any other offerings.

There are certain conditions - such as prolonged periods of low water and hot weather - when, at dusk, and again at dawn, this surface fishing for sewin is the only productive method. T. L.'s Sedge, like the modern Muddler Minnow, is then just the right tool for the job.

T. L. Harries was not himself an enthusiastic flydresser. He was, however, a great innovator - responsible for cross-pollinating ideas from rivers like the Towy and the Teifi, the Usk and the Cothi. It is thought that patterns like T.L.s Sedge were probably tied by that great Lampeter flytyer, Fred Atkins. Many of Wil Harry's creations also were in his well-worn leather fly-wallet when he died in 1951.

Torby Coch

PLATE 4

Hook: 6 & 8
Tying silk: Yellow
Rib: Flat tinsel
Tail: Red ibis (substitute)
Body: Light coloured hare's ear
Hackle: Brown hen
Wing: Plain brown hen

Another fly from the Conway which came to prominence some thirty years ago is the Torby Coch. It has many big sewin to its credit and is a favourite with anglers in the Dolwyddelan area.

Despite the modern swing towards sewin flies with silver tinsel bodies, the old fur and fibre bodied flies remain supreme for daytime fishing when the water is low.

A number of traditional sewin flies have fur bodies: this light fawn has undoubtedly proved itself attractive. It is puzzling why some patterns are effective on certain rivers and then fail miserably on others. The Torby

Coch has proved its value on the Dwyfawr, Glaslyn and the Ystwyth. One angler who has done well with the Torby Coch ties it well up on the cast as a dropper.

Towy Topper

PLATE 4

Hook: 8 & 10
Tying silk: Black
Tail: Golden pheasant tippets
Rib: Thin silver wire
Body: Well marked quill
Hackle: Blue dun or rusty dun

The river Towy is a wonderful sewin river and it is not surprising that so many seatrout patterns have been developed and perfected there. The Towy Topper is not as well known now as other patterns, but it still has its admirers, especially amongst daytime anglers.

The day angler can fish the Towy Topper in the runs and shadows of trees and take sewin even during low water conditions. Sewin will, in summer levels, tend to move into the more oxygenated rush and the Towy Topper is at its best at times like these, fished small and fine. Fished as a size 12 dry-fly the Towy Topper has also proved successful for stale fish. This method, especially just as dawn is breaking, can be very rewarding.

Treble Chance

PLATE 5

Hook: Waddington iron one to three inches long
Tying silk: Black
Body: Flat gold
Rib: Gold wire
Wing: Grey squirrel

It is a simple pattern to tie and is best dressed on a fairly slim Twiggy-like form, as one angler described it. The natural squirrel tail needs to be well marked in order to give the wing a good colour pattern. Squirrel tail hair makes perfect wing for this pattern as its texture is ideal for providing the life and movement so necessary in fishing deep, still pools. The red fluorescent varnish at head and tail adds trigger points to the pattern.

The fly has something of a reputation for taking big fish. On the Rheidol, Malcolm Edwards, doyen of sewin anglers, took one sewin of 16lbs 8ozs and another of 12lbs on the Treble Chance in the 1991 season. Malcolm favours a Treble Chance dressed on a one-inch Waddington iron and fishes it on a sink tip line.

When sewin are in a frivolous mood and seem to be playing tip-and-run with anglers' offerings, anglers experience a series of abortive plucks, and it is then that a small treble on the tail can prove deadly. Some experienced anglers, like Glyn Jones of Gwyryd Hotel fishery on the Conwy, favour Treble Chance dressed on small single hooks. He demonstrated its effectiveness when we shared an evening recently on the famous Beaver Pool.

Twm Twll

PLATE 4

Hook: 8 & 10
Tying silk: Yellow
Tail: A blue hackle tip
Rib: Gold wire thread
Body: Hare's ear and orange wool mixed
Hackle: Rusty Andulusian cock

This fly is dressed very lightly with the minimum of materials. It was created by T. L. Harries, the auctioneer from Lampeter. T.L. was a great trout angler who, no doubt, brought his restrained, upper-Teifi approach to sewin fishing.

The Twm Twll is a very delicate fly, similar to the Dai Ben - except that it has a much darker tone. It can be used effectively in conjunction with Dai Ben. The Dai Ben, with its lighter tone and thick silver rib, is recommended for use in the early part of the season when the fish are fresh in the river. The Twm Twll should be used later on in the season.

Wasp Fly

PLATE 3

Hook: 12 (Salmon size)
Tying silk: Brown
Tail: Three mauve fibres
Butt: Black ostrich
Body: Peacock herl
Rib: Yellow orange floss
Wing: Rich brown speckled hen

Another dressing which originated in the nineteenth century from Francis Francis. Its modern version is still useful for both sewin and salmon.

Water Rat & Red

PLATE 4

Hook: 9 & 12
Tying silk: Black
Tail: Dark red cock
Rib: Silver wire
Body: Water rat fur
Hackle: Dark red cock
Wing: Corncrake (substitute speckled hen)

Another fly from the box of Dr Shelton Roberts which has stood the test of time over the last half century, as a daytime fly in low water. Cotton's advice in *The Compleat Angler* 'to fine and far off' is operative with the Water Rat & Red. The bigger version tied on a number nine hook has a wider silver band on it; the number twelve hook is preferred when the water is very low.

North Wales sewin flies are similar to those used for trout fishing on lakes and rivers. This pattern is the exception, being a modification of an established Irish pattern. There is a long history in angling, of coming and going between Ireland and North Wales - due to proximity and the similarity of conditions in peaty waters (which do not apply in south west and south east Wales).

White Owl

PLATE 2

Francis Francis describes a fly called the 'White Owl' which was literally white all over like a barn owl. It was a fly to be used all night for, with the coming of dawn, he observes, the fish 'cease biting'.

Wil Harry's Green Woodcock

PLATE 4

Hook: 8 & 10
Tying silk: Green
Tail: Golden pheasant tippets
Rib: Gold wire
Body: Light olive green seal's fur
Hackle: Woodcock
Wing: Woodcock

This fly is dressed very much in sedge form with bulky body and a heavy hackle and wing. Its body has a distinctive green shade, identical to that used in Ireland for the great Green Peter.

Sedge fishing for sewin is often practised when the water is running high. Under such conditions night fishing is not productive and anglers fish to the lip of the evening - just before the daylight is lost.

This pattern, which was originally for sewin fishing on the river Towy, has the added ingredient of being an exceptional sedge pattern. It has similarities with the G & H Sedge (Goddard and Henry) and deserves a fair trial purely as a trout fly.

Worm Fly

PLATE 5

Hook: Two number 6 or 8
Tying silk: Black
Tail: Red wool
Rib: Gold wire
Body: Peacock herl
Hackle: Coch-a-bon-ddu

The idea of joining two Coch-a-bon-ddu is a comparatively new one as a reservoir lure but it has been around a long time as a 'poacher's fly'. There is a modern tendency to use most reservoir lures right on the bottom. The Worm Fly, however, is often used as a bob fly. The two-hook principle was intended to help with hooking (bob flies are notorious for their poor hooking capability).

An interesting development in the use of the Worm Fly has been its use on an intermediate line. This could well be the most important role for the Worm Fly. The intermediate fly line is of neutral density and allows fishing just below the surface film. The Worm Fly in the smaller sizes dressed on two No 10 hooks has proved very effective at dawn. It is certainly at its best when fished slowly.

The origin of the Worm Fly is still something of a mystery, but as it is made of two Coch-a-bon-ddu flies it is reasonable to suppose that it could have been developed somewhere in the Principality.

Yellow Plasterer

PLATE 5

Hook: 8 & 10
Tying silk: Yellow
Tail: Red fibres
Body: Yellow plastic
Hackle: Woodcock

A very colourful fly devised in the 1950s by Lewi Davies who was a plasterer in the Llandeilo area. The plastic strips give a very useful impression of a segmented body and the strong yellow gives high visibility on rivers such as the Towy. As the plastic used on the Lewi's original fly was rather heavy, there is little doubt that it was intended to sink rapidly to fish deeply, and would be well suited to fishing the deep glides of the middle reaches of the Llandeilo Association and old Dynevor Estate waters where Lewi fished.

Use of the modern swannundaze for the body gives a smoother effect for the body segmentation than Lewi achieved with his yellow plastic strips. This refinement could prove counter-productive for it is often those roughly-tied flies that prove to be as he would say, 'the killers': just as flies that have been knocked almost to pieces with catching fish are often more effective than newly-tied 'exhibition' examples.

127

The Salmon Flies

It is now commonly accepted that the salmon does not feed in freshwater and therefore he takes the fly either out of curiosity, aggression or memory. As to exactly what the salmon fly is supposed to represent to him and whether the 'fly' has any resemblance to items of food is anyone's guess - and actually immaterial. A great number of traditional feather-wing flies are tied merely as an aesthetic exercise and their dressers would not think of fishing with them. Quite apart from its use as a catcher of fish, the correctly dressed salmon fly is a work of art.

The earliest reference to the salmon fly appears in *The Booke of St Albans*. In that collection of manuscripts by various hands, Dame Juliana Berners in her *Treatyse of Fysshynge Wyth an Angle* observes that when a salmon leaps, it is possible to take him with a fly. In the mid-seventeenth century Thomas Barker, who caught salmon in the Thames, outlined the construction of the salmon fly, which, according to his authority, had four wings. It was not until the early nineteenth century that flyfishing became the socially accepted way of fishing for salmon and the flies then in use for their pursuit were inclined to be of a sombre hue.

George Agar Hansard writing in 1834 about Welsh salmon flies tells us: 'The flies used by the native Welsh angler are very sober in colour and few in number. The hooks they prefer are also large and the execution altogether exceedingly coarse!'

A Spring Fly:
Wings, the dark mottled feathers of the bittern, body orange silk or worsted with broad gold twist and a smokey dun hackle for legs'.

129

A Summer Fly:
Wings, the brown mottled feather of a turkey cock's wing with a few of
the green strands selected from the eye of a peacock tail feather. Body
of yellow silk, and gold twist, with deep blood-red hackle for legs.'

At the same time, so-called 'Irish flies' were being sold in the shops of the
seaports of Wales. Within twenty years, these imported flies, with their
colourful feathers had been responsible for the capture of many hundreds of
Welsh salmon. Hansard gives one dressing of an Irish salmon fly:

'The wings were made of the feathers of a guineafowl; the body of a
blood red ostrich feather and the hackle of yellow and blood red
feathers.'

In 1845 the most famous salmon fly of all time was tied - the Jock Scott. It
was first dressed by a Scottish ghillie on board ship on the North Sea - bound
for Scandinavia. It was tied for a Scottish gentleman names Scott. It is not
known for certain if the first Jock Scott was dressed on a metal-eyed hook
even though the first metal-eyed hook was produced in that same year.

Following the advent of the Jock Scott, salmon flies changed their garb
completely. It meant an end to the dull, sombre colours and into fashion
came the exotic colours of tropical birds. The blue and green parrot, blue and
yellow macaw, red and gold of the golden pheasant and the black, yellow and
white of the jungle cock became the rage. Ireland, too, played a prominent
part in this revolution and the 'Irish flies' were being widely sold in tackle
shops at the seaports - the name of Rogan of Ballyshannon becoming familiar
on Welsh rivers.

Despite the invention of the metal-eyed hook in 1845, Welsh anglers were
observed still to be using the gut eye on their salmon flies as late as the
1890s. An interesting collection of salmon flies of that period is now housed
in Llanllyr Mansion in the Vale of Aeron. Captain Hext Lewes has a fly-book
which was used by both his father and grandfather containing the flies in use
during their two lifetimes in the last century on the upper stretches of the
river Wye - with very comprehensive notes attached. Most of the flies in the
collection have vivid yellow bodies and the notes reveal that most of the flies
were reckoned to be effective during the months of September and October.
The late John Lewes records the capture of six salmon in one morning on a
visit to the Highmead Beat on the river Teifi. All was not well, even in those

days, with salmon stocks - as an entry in the accompanying notes says that in the year 1898 the fishing was so poor that it was not worth the price paid for the licence!

A page in the old wallet reveals that all the salmon flies tied for the Nantegwyllt estate on the Upper Wye were dressed on what would now be considered big hooks.

Since the first decade of this century, the dressing of salmon flies in Wales has been moving back towards its earlier form. In 1920 A.H.E. Wood convinced many anglers of the necessity of using smaller, more sparsely-dressed flies near the surface of the water. In the forties and fifties it was becoming acknowledged that hair-wing flies were steadily growing in usefulness displacing the feathered, fully-dressed, traditional varieties. The influence was largely from the United States.

These American hairwinged flies, tied with limited materials and skills, were rather crude. Yet they proved effective. They were made from deer hair, fox fur and squirrel tails. Success with patterns such as the Stoat's Tail hastened the end of the fully-dressed salmon fly, added to which there was the increasing difficulty of getting the correct feathers for some of the Scottish and Irish patterns. So, the salmon fly has gone the complete circle, and modern anglers are almost back to where it all started nearly four hundred years ago - tying effective flies from simple, durable materials readily to hand.

Black Doctor

PLATE 6

Hook: 6 & 8
Tying silk: Black
Tag: Round Silver tinsel and lemon floss
Tail: Topping and Indian crow
Butt: Scarlet wool
Body: Black floss
Rib: Oval tinsel
Hackle: Dark claret hackle
Throat Speckled guinea fowl
Wings: Mixed - Tippet in strands with golden pheasant tail over married strands of scarlet, blue and yellow goose, florican bustard, peacock wings and light mottled turkey tail, married narrow strips of teal and barred summer duck, narrow strips of brown mallard over and topping over all
Head: Scarlet wool

The Doctor series of salmon flies was formerly much in use on many Welsh rivers such as the Towy, Wye, Cleddau and the Usk. In the early nineteenth century, even on the Cothi, a tributary of the Towy, the Black Doctor was considered to be the right medicine for the Autumn running salmon.

Early examples of Doctor salmon flies were tied with gut eyes, despite the fact that after 1845 metal eyed hooks were available. Salmon anglers were rather conservative in their approach and distrusted innovation, feeling that the gut-to-gut tyings fished better.

Blue Doctor

PLATE 6

Hook: 6 & 8
Tying silk: Black
Tag: Round silver thread and golden yellow floss
Tail: A topping and a tippet
Butt: Scarlet wool
Body: Pale blue floss
Ribs: Oval silver tinsel
Hackle: Pale blue hackle
Throat: Pale blue hackle
Throat: Blue jay
Wings: Mixed - tippets in strands with strip of golden pheasant tail over married strands of scarlet blue and yellow swan, florican bustard, peacock wing and light mottled turkey tail, married narrow strips of teal and barred summer duck, narrow strips of brown mallard over, a topping over all
Head: Scarlet wool

The Blue Doctor did not gain quite such a reputation on Welsh rivers as did the Black and Silver Doctors, but when it was discovered that it was also a good sewin fly, the situation changed dramatically. The Blue Doctor became extremely active on the lower Teifi at the turn of the century but it was to give way to the Silver Doctor in later years.

Silver Doctor

PLATE 6

Hook: 6 & 8
Tying silk: Black
Tag: Round silver tinsel and golden yellow floss
Tail: A topping and blue chatterer
Butt: Scarlet wool
Body: Flat silver tinsel
Ribs: Fine oval silver thread
Throat: A pale blue hackle and wigeon
Wings: Mixed - tippet in strands with strips of golden pheasant tail over married strands of scarlet, blue and yellow swan or goose, florican, bustard, peacock wing and light mottled turkey tail, married narrow strips of teal and barred summer duck, narrow strips of brown mallard over, a topping over all
Head: Scarlet wool

The Silver Doctor was considered, on the

upper Usk, a good early season fly, dressed in bigger sizes. The three members of the Doctor series, Black, Silver and Blue, were standbys for many anglers and, when the complicated Scottish built-wing patterns fell out of use, these three patterns quickly took on their simple, hair-wing garb.

Conway Blue

PLATE 6

Hook: 6 & 8
Tying silk: Dark blue
Tag: Round silver thread and golden yellow floss
Tail: Golden pheasant crest
Butt: Black ostrich herl
Rib: Oval silver tinsel
Body: Royal blue seal's fur
Hackles: Black hackle, dyed blue cock
Front hackle: Blue jay
Wing: Two golden pheasant tippet feathers tied back-to-back
Roof: Bronze mallard with golden pheasant topping over it

The Conway Blue is a highly colourful pattern which works well on the rivers Conway, Dee and Dovey. The importance of visibility is largely historical - recalling a time in the salmon's life as a predator in flashing Arctic waters, and harking back to times in angling history before the fixed spool reel made life difficult for the salmon, if easier for the unimaginative angler.

J.O. Jones of Llanrwst was one of the leading anglers in North Wales during the 1930s and 40s and he was fortunate to have fished for salmon on the river Conway when it held really good stocks of salmon. He fished the salmon fly on a silk line in mid-water. Most salmon fishing was done in those days immediately after a flood and salmon flies were used in conditions which are now reserved for the spinning minnow and its ferrous relatives.

J.O. Jones was fond of his pattern and he maintained that it would also do well at the tail end of the season when the smaller sewin came upriver. Another prominent salmon angler in North Wales, R.H. Hughes who was an enthusiast for the Conway Blue, gave the pattern to Tom Stewart for his book, *Two Hundred Popular Fly Patterns*. Hughes dressed most of his flies on the slim side and was most economical with his materials. His slim version was most effective in low water conditions of high summer.

Dwyryd Red & Yellow

PLATE 6

Hook: 6 & 8
Tying silk: Black
Tail: Golden pheasant topping
Body: Rear third, yellow wool; Middle third, red wool; Front third, black wool
Hackle: Guinea fowl
Wing: Dark brown turkey

This was an attempt to follow the trend towards bright colourings that overtook salmon fly-dressers at the end of the last century. Most of their materials were home-produced and the overall attempt of the fly design was to imitate Scottish and Irish patterns. Salmon fishing was not widely practised by the locals during the 19th century and so salmon fly patterns were not subject to as much experimentation as were trout flies.

The Dwyryd river has a fair run of summer salmon and in the Maentwrog area it lends itself well to fly fishing. Most fly fishing activity takes place when the river is running down after a flood and the brightly coloured body is ideal in the brown-stained water.

Some reports of quite astounding catches - five or six fish to one rod in an hour - are recorded on the Dwyryd river and

133

there is little doubt that when the river is at the correct level, the fly is as deadly a method as any.

Haslam

PLATE 6

Hook: 6 & 8
Tying silk: Black
Tag: Flat silver tinsel
Butt: White wool or floss
Tail: Small golden pheasant crest
Body: Flat silver tinsel
Body: Oval silver wire
Throat hackle: Blue jay, or guinea fowl dyed blue
Horns: Blue macaw, curving along the wings and crossing over the tail
Wing: Hen pheasant tail
Head: Black varnish

Old examples of the Haslam tied on gut-loop eyes are still in existence. This killing pattern is attributed to Sam Haslam of Uppingham, now famed for founding the excellent fishery at Rutland reservoir. But it is doubtful if Sam Haslam is accountable for introducing the pattern to Wales, and to the river Dovey in particular, which is acknowledged as its Welsh home.

Peter Vaughan, a tackle dealer at Machynlleth on the river Dovey, was the man largely responsible for spreading the fame of the Haslam of which he sold literally thousands in a season. Peter Vaughan claimed that it was by far the best fly to use for salmon on the Dovey and that it worked equally well in low or high water conditions. Such was its effectiveness that it was known also as 'The Universal Provider'.

The Haslam could be effective also in small sizes, as a sewin fly. In the Dovey area anglers call all seatrout up to one pound 'sewin' and anything over that weight 'seatrout'. This distinction is not made in any other part of Wales.

Somehow over the years the Haslam pattern developed body hackle. Most samples sold by Peter Vaughan in the forties had white body hackles. There is no doubt that this did add to the attractiveness of the fly.

The version tied by George Roberts, doyen of Dovey anglers, has hackle right through the body. The variation tied by Amos had a much darker hue. The variations attributed to George Forrest, Billy Mitchell and Jim Dulson, all expert Dovey anglers, also show slight bias towards the darker end of the spectrum. The pattern sold by Mrs Aylward in the tackle shop in Machynlleth has a false blue jay hackle and an orange tag. The popular sizes are six and eight.

Irt Fly

PLATE 6

Hook: 4 & 5
Tying silk: Black
Tag: Flat silver
Tail: Golden pheasant toppings
Rib: Silver thread
Body: Two turns of red silk, rest of blue tinsel
Hackle: Black, orange
Wing: Squirrel tail dyed red orange

This fly has an excellent reputation on the river Lledr which is a tributary of the Conway. It is extremely colourful and does well in spate conditions. Eirwyn Roberts of Dolwyddelan, a fine dresser of salmon flies, dresses the Irt fly for some of his friends. It would seem that the success it scores on the Lledr river is not general. Extensive trials on the Usk and Severn by a number of anglers have not brought many good results.

The Irt fly has also been quite successful on the river Rheidol on a few occasions, catching fresh sewin just off the tidal stretch of the river.

Jenny Wren *(Pluen y Dryw)*

PLATE 7

Hook: 7
Tying silk: Brown
Tail: Golden pheasant topping and mallard
Rib: Silver tinsel
Body: Dark hare's ear
Hackle: Dark red cock and brown partridge
Wing: Medium mallard over grey goose feather

This modestly-dressed little fly, used by Dr Shelton Roberts some fifty years ago, was effective on the rivers of North Wales - especially the Dwyfawr. The bias in North Wales is towards browns and greys as opposed to the colourful creations used on the Dee, Wye and Usk.

The normal method of fishing the Dwyfawr is the downriver wet fly for salmon which run strongly in mid summer. The salmon clearly go for the smaller, more drab fly which they often take just below the surface: the rather bulky body tending to hold the Jenny Wren high in the water.

Jock Scott

PLATE 7

Hook: 4 & 6
Tying silk: Black
Butt: Black herl
Body: In two equal halves - first half golden yellow floss butted with black herl and veiled above and below with six or more toucan feathers; second half black floss
Rib: Fine oval silver tinsel over golden yellow floss, broader oval silver tinsel or flat silver tinsel and twist over black floss
Hackle: A black hackle over black floss
Throat: Speckled gallina
Wings: A pair of black white-tipped turkey tail strips; over these, but not entirely covering them, a mixed sheath of married strands of peacock wing, yellow, scarlet and blue swan, bustard, florican and golden pheasant tail; two strands of peacock sword feathers above the married narrow strips of teal and barred summer duck at the sides, brown mallard over
Sides: Jungle cock
Cheeks: Blue chatterer
Horns: Blue and yellow macaw. A topping over all

This is without doubt one of the best known salmon fly patterns of all times. Little did the fisherman who first devised this complicated pattern realise that he was to achieve immortality with it. The year of its birth was 1845, when Jock Scott was en route to Norway with his employer, Lord John Scott. He tied the fly on the journey. It proved to be an excellent pattern in Scotland and its fame spread quickly to other rivers. In Wales it has scored well on the Dee, Wye and Usk.

The Jock Scott is one of the most difficult patterns to dress - even the modern version of it with hair wings. Both versions are equally effective.

It will be a sad day for the art of fly dressing when the old patterns like the Jock Scott are no longer being tied anywhere - even as an exercise in dexterity and craftsmanship.

Leslie Peters

PLATE 7

Hook: 6 & 8
Tying silk: Yellow
Tail: Golden pheasant toppings. Black silk
Rib: Golden wire
Body: Yellow seal's fur
Hackle: Yellow hackle
Wing: Grey squirrel dyed brown or off-black

In recent years most salmon fly patterns have been simplified and the former Jock

Scott that needed twenty six different items for its original tying, now in its hair-wing form, only requires nine. This simplication of patterns has also been in evidence on Welsh rivers where hair-winged salmon flies are now used extensively.

Leslie Peters of Brecon, who has fished the river Usk for over fifty years, has developed this hair-wing salmon fly which he now uses in preference to the old fully-built winged salmon flies. The highly-visible yellow seal's fur body is in keeping with the traditional salmon flies used on the Usk in Brecon around 1850 which can be seen in a case at Brecon Museum today. The wing for the fly is dyed squirrel tail and the whole pattern is simple to tie and not expensive to make.

Penybont

Plate 7

Hook: 6 & 8
Tying silk: Yellow
Tail: Golden pheasant tippets
Rib: Silver thread
Body: Well waxed yellow silk
Hackle: Brown hen
Wing: Grey heron wing, encasing golden pheasant tippets

This is a rather sober-coloured fly which some anglers on the upper Dovey use as a dropper with the more colourful Haslam on the point. The choice of size would be governed by the flow of the river. The river Dovey has a big catchment area and is subject to quite big, and prolonged, flood conditions. The Penybont is effective when the water is thinning down.

One somewhat unusual method of fishing the Penybont is to use it as a point fly. After tying it on in the normal manner, loop the nylon back around its throat. This is then cast across the river and the eye of the hook is kept in the surface film of the water, just like a miniature periscope. Salmon hooked by fishing this method are always fast by the top of the mouth. The fly is best tied on a double hook if it is intended to fish this way, and well worth a try using other patterns, in pools of slow to medium flow and when the water temperatures are up to summer level.

Some versions of this fly are tied (minus the golden tipppets) in smaller sizes for summer fishing. Sometimes the body is made of dirty yellow seal's fur and the brown hackle is palmered down the body. In this guise it is also attractive to sewin.

Pry llwyd a choch
(Badger hair & red)

Plate 7

Hook: 6 & 8
Tying silk: Black
Tag: Flat silver
Tail: Golden pheasant toppings
Rib: Red tinsel
Body: Black seal's fur
Hackle: Badger
Wing: Badger hair

This fly, although primarily a salmon fly, is also used extensively for sewin fishing.

As with many fly patterns, the amount of dressing used can influence the method of fishing the fly. When dressed fully, it is best used as a normal wet fly on a sinking or sink-tip line. Used in this fashion on the quick-flowing rivers of North Wales, it takes fish that have just moved into the river or are on the move from pool to pool.

A slimmer version can be fished with the fly in or very near the surface. This method, which has been compared to nymph fishing in a reservoir, is effective with salmon that have been in the river for some time.

Richard's Fancy

PLATE 7

Hook: 8 & 10 single or double Limerick
Tying silk: Black
Tail: Golden Pheasant topping
Body: Black floss
Rib: Flat gold tinsel
Hackle: Blue dun
Wing: Bronze mallard

Dilwyn Richards is the natural successor to Wil Harry Richards and Lewi Davies in that he learned at an early age the art of innovation derived from his observations. Dilwyn's early lessons were absorbed while fishing the fly-only Dynevor and Cawdor waters on the Towy at Llandeilo. The sight of an insect with a particular blue wing which rose several salmon on one occasion sent him back to his work-bench one day in the mid-seventies. Within a couple of hours he was back, and soon had a brace of fish on the bank. This is an approach in defiance of the many pundits who have written about salmon fishing maintaining that a salmon 'take' is pure reflex to some deep-sea memory that makes the fish move to a fly. Those who have observed as closely as Dilwyn Richards has, will know that salmon will sometimes rise like a trout and can even sometimes be seen in slack water with their backs out of the water as if nymphing.

The salmon's formative year is lived as a trout in brooks and rivers when it will take small flies avidly. This youthful memory must remain with them when they return to their native streams on migration, and I am convinced that this is why they will sometimes come up to a dry fly.

Stoat's Tail

PLATE 7

Hook: 6
Tying silk: Black
Tail: Golden pheasant topping
Rib: Silver thread
Body: Black seal's fur
Hackle: Black hen
Wing: Black tip of stoat's tail or black bucktail

This is now one of the most commonly used salmon flies and has for some time been used to good effect on the Usk and the Wye and to a lesser extent on the river Dee. There are minor variations observable in the dressing from river to river depending on local availability of materials. In recent years the Stoat's Tail wing has given way to bucktail wing which, according to some, appears to be more effective.

This fly is generally tied as a tube fly or a Waddington these days - the reason for this is the alleged greater hooking power of the treble. A number of anglers on the rivers of mid Wales use stainless wire to build the body upon and then attach a treble hook to the end. These home-made traces are very effective and very cheap. The great advantage of making one's own trace is that it is possible to add different weights to it - enabling the fly to be fished at the required depth.

Thunder & Lightning

PLATE 8

Hook: 6
Tying silk: Black
Tag: Round gold tinsel, yellow floss silk
Tail: Golden pheasant topping
Butt: Black ostrich herl
Body: Black floss silk ribbed with gold tinsel
Hackle: Orange

Throat hackle: Blue jay
Wings: Bronze mallard and golden pheasant toppings
Cheeks: Jungle cock

This is one of the most frequently-used salmon flies on Welsh rivers and its dark hues suit the peat-stained waters of Wales. Of all the popular salmon flies this is one of the easiest to dress, and it bears quite a close relationship to the old Welsh 'Turkey' flies. It is also one pattern that can be dressed in various forms without losing any of its effectiveness. The demand in recent years for the use of the treble hook in preference to the single has seen this pattern dressed as a tube fly, Waddington and on Esmond Drury hooks. Some anglers on the lower Teifi use Thunder & Lightning as a low water pattern and it is a style of dressing that does well towards the evening of a warm day in summer when the small summer salmon or grisle have started running.

On the principle of a bright fly for bright day, this dark pattern does better than most others in water that is heavily stained after flood. Some Welsh rivers that run out of peaty moors tend to give anglers a couple of days sport in beer-coloured water, not the best of water for success; but this is the very type of water that favours this particular pattern.

In tying this simple salmon fly, it is probably advisable to use a matched pair of mallard feathers for the wing. Many dressers use double matched pairs, which makes for a more solidly-built dressing. Some insist that it is imperative to make a red head with varnish.

This pattern was created by that excellent salmon flydresser from Sprouston on the Tweed, James Wright. It was first tied around the 1850s when fully-dressed salmon flies were at the height of vogue.

Twrci Coch *(Red Turkey)*

PLATE 8

Hook: 6
Tying silk: Black
Tag: Silver thread and yellow silk
Tail: Golden pheasant toppings with red feather
Rib: Gold thread
Body: Hare's fur
Hackle: Ginger cock
Throat hackle: Blue jay
Wing: Brown turkey

This salmon fly is a native of North Wales and has accounted for a good number of salmon on the river Conway. It first saw light of day in the forties and, curiously, it has not proved its effectiveness in other areas.

In its original form it was dressed rather heavily, although some have tended to dress a slimmer and smaller version in the last decade. It was formerly considered to be an especially good grilse fly, and, as grisle runs have tended to diminish in recent years, so the reputation of the fly has suffered accordingly. The Twrci Coch was also a favourite fly on the river Dee, but in a darker version which first became popular in the late twenties.

Twrci Du *(Black Turkey)*

PLATE 8

Hook: 6
Tying silk: Black
Body: Black wool and black seal's fur
Tag: Silver thread and yellow silk
Tail: Golden pheasant toppings with red feather
Rib: Gold thread
Body: Hare's fur
Hackle: Ginger cock
Throat hackle: Blue jay

Wing: Brown turkey

Some anglers who fished between Bala and Corwen found this fly a better pattern than the original. The sole variation is the black wool and black seals' fur for the body. G.O. Jones of Llanrwst was of the opinion that black was a good colour to use on summer salmon. He likened this pattern to the better-known Thunder & Lightning and considered the salmon angler who did not have either the Twrci Du or Thunder & Lightning on him to be improperly dressed!

Usk Grub

PLATE 8

Hook: 4 & 6
Tying silk: Black
Tag: Silver thread
Rear hackle: Golden pheasant red plumage
Body: Rear half, dull orange
Hackle: (halfway down hook) White and orange
Body: Front half, black seal's fur
Rib: Silver thread
Front hackle: Pair of jungle cock

Many inexperienced anglers confuse this pattern with the Welsh Shrimp Fly which is rather similar. This confusion seldom takes place on the river Usk where the Usk Grub has long been a firm favourite. The fully-dressed version has been somewhat trimmed down and it appears that the simpler modern version is equally effective when the salmon are in the river in good numbers.

This pattern was a speciality of the late Molly Sweet who used to dress salmon and trout flies for local and visiting anglers fishing the river Usk. It was joy to watch her create a very neat fly because the Usk Grub can often look a very bedraggled specimen when dressed by flydressers of lesser ability. Her square-headed vice was especially well-suited to dress this pattern particularly

when tied on a double hook. The version tied by Molly Sweet was a much fuller and more bulky fly than that dressed by Captain Coombe Richards whose version of the Usk Grub was far more slim-line and bordering on a low-water version.

The Sweet family of Usk were the ideal fishing couple in that Molly dressed killing patterns for both trout and salmon and Lionel, her husband, used them with great precision and delicacy to take fish from the nearest river.

Welsh Shrimp Fly

PLATE 8

Hook: 6 & 8
Tying silk: Yellow
Tag: Yellow floss
Tail: Golden pheasant crest feather
Butt: Black ostrich herl
Body: Yellow floss
Rib: Oval silver tinsel
Wing: Tip of a red golden pheasant body feather tied over body of fly with jungle cock each side
Hackle: White cock wound as a collar
Head: Black varnish

The late J.O Jones, Llanwrst, a noted angler on the lower reaches of the river Conway, was responsible for this pattern, which grew up and developed on the river Conway, becoming widely known and adopted on the salmon rivers that flow into what is now called the Celtic Sea.

'J.O.' as he was known to his friends, used the sinking line for most of his salmon fishing. He would favour this pattern dressed rather full on a size six hook. Many anglers now use the Welsh Shrimp Fly in much smaller sizes and find it effective as a low-water pattern.

Salmon fishing on the Conway was at its best when the river was thinning down after a flood. In the days when J.O. operated, the river took the best part of a week to thin down - which resulted in long periods of ideal all-round wet-fly fishing conditions. The fact that this is a colourful pattern was of help when fresh-run salmon moved in the wake of a flood.

In recent years, a variation on the Welsh Shrimp has come into being and is probably now more widely used than its predecessor.

Welsh Shrimp Fly (variant)

PLATE 8

Hook: 8
Tying silk: Yellow
Tail: Reddish golden pheasant body fibres
Rib: Silver thread
Body: Rear two thirds, yellow floss. Front third, black floss
Hackle: Body hackle at joint of body, badger cock
Front hackle: Orange
Wing: Two short jungle cock tied back to back

The variation is used in identical conditions and like manner. It is often tied on double hooks and has gained favour with salmon anglers on the river Dwyryd.

Wil Harry

PLATE 8

Hook: 4 & 6
Tying silk: Black
Tag: Silver thread
Tail: Peacock sword feather
Rib: Silver wire
Body: Rear third, orange wool; Front part, black silk
Hackle: Olive cock
Wing: Blue and red swan with peacock herl

This interesting Towy salmon fly, which was the creation of William Henry Richards of Llandeilo, is as good an example of a local

pattern as one would wish to find. Wil Harry, who worked as a carpenter on the Dynevor estate, was an immensely personable character who breathed and lived fishing. It appears that even in the most heated moments of the Battle of the Somme, when Wil served with the Royal Engineers, he found time to go fishing behind the lines. He claimed, as a boy, to have been inveigled into Sunday School attendance only twice. On the first occasion he saw the feathers in the teacher's hat, and on the second occasion when he got them. Could this have been the imaginative birth-place of this iridescent fly?

The Wil Harry is a colourful pattern which ensures that it is highly visible under difficult light conditions and attractive in fast-moving water. It deserves tying on double and treble hooks and being more widely used: it has a pleasing simplicity about it and the 'lethal' appearance of a really good salmon fly.

Index

141

Materials

Flydressers today are very fortunate in that they have a wide range of specialist firms eager to supply them with dressing materials and who issue comprehensive catalogues for them to study, ensuring that they get the best materials at the right price. It was not always so. Even the most casual survey of fishing tackle catalogues of 40 years ago will show that interest was more concentrated on ready-tied patterns and the colour-plates of popular patterns were much prized and, no doubt, very persuasive to the buyer. Prior to that, those 'amateurs' who tied their own flies had to use ready-to-hand materials or scratch around for anything unusual.

There are some excellent stories about the lengths to which some of the old tyers went, to obtain the materials they wanted, none nicer than the one which claims to be the true account of the origin of the Bethesda fly (Cochen-lady) where a quarry worker-fisherman saw the exact dubbing wool he needed seated opposite him on a train. When they entered a tunnel he made a dive at her shawl, amidst considerable protest and confusion!

Some materials readily available forty years ago are no longer obtainable because of changing times and man's depredations. The introduction of mechanised hay-mowers has meant the extinction of a once-common summer bird in Wales, the corncrake. The lack of need for self-sufficiency has meant that for the most part, few Welsh farmers bother with cereal crops and so those lovely birds, the partridges,have disappeared together with the bitterns, nightjars, wrynecks and others - not to mention the otter and the red squirrel.

Let it be noted well from the outset that many of these birds and animals mentioned in the text are referred to strictly as historical illuminations. It is not, and this cannot be stressed too strongly, for anyone to even think of trying to obtain any of these feathers, in the vain hope that it might improve their chances of taking fish. The substitutes suggested are equally good in every case and the penalties for taking, or even disturbing, some of these protected species are severe. Apart from this, it would be an act of the gravest irresponsibly, even to contemplate.

Most traditional Welsh patterns used hackles from either a hen or a cock. Traditionally hen hackle was used to dress wet flies and cock hackle for dry flies. Some cock hackles are becoming difficult to obtain as the old farm rooster has become something of an endangered species himself. Many believe that it is essential for the cock to be three years old before his hackle is of the correct texture for the dry fly. This is not so. Many of the old lads who bred fighting cocks in the valleys could produce a fully mature cock from the point of view of hackle and strength in a matter of eighteen months.

Often it is difficult to obtain hackle of the exact right colour: natural colours such as coch-a-bon-ddu and various honey dun requirements are very scarce. Fortunately, great strides have been made in the dyeing of feathers and even the most delicate of shades can be achieved - with a little care.

As a beginner the fly dresser will find it difficult to recognise the various hackles. The following is a simple glossary description of the more commonly used hackles:

Coch-a-bon-ddu Black centre with red outer fibres with black tips.
Furnace Black centre with red outer fibres.
Badger Black centre with white outer fibres
Grizzle A feather from a Plymouth Rock bird with bars of black and white alternately.
Cree A feather with ginger added to the normal Plymouth Rock colour.
Greenwell Black centre with ginger outer fibres.
Blue Dun The colour of an old Welsh slate.
Iron Blue Dun A dark shade of blue dun
Dun A mousey grey colour
Honey or Rusty Dun A dun feather with rusty or honey coloured tips.

Modern dressers have resorted to the use of felt pens to help them with patterns requiring coch-a-bon-ddu and furnace hackle; the use of photo-dyeing has provided blue duns of astounding quality. Thus, despite modern dressers lacking the genuine article, there are modern devices to help them out. Many birds other than domestic poultry can supply out-moded hackle. The partridge and snipe are valuable in this respect even though these birds may be better known for providing the material for winging flies.

Wild Duck
An extremely useful bird and plentiful. The bronze mallard feather - from the small of the back - is much in demand for dressing the Mallard series of flies. The best bronze feathers are obtainable in the early months of the year as the mallard drake comes into mating plumage.

Those secondary feathers on a mallard duck and drake's wing that have a bright blue sheen on them are essential for the Butcher series flies.

Grouse
The tail and secondary feathers are used for wings in the Grouse series. The feathers from the small of the back can be used as hackles for flies such as Dai Lewis's Alder.

Partridge
The wing of the partridge is used on a great number of patterns in the Bethesda area. Partridge tail feathers are used to make the wing of the March Brown. The hackle from the small of the back are used for all the Partridge series of flies that require the dark brown hackle, such as the Partridge Red and Partridge Purple. The grey partridge breast feather is used for the lighter coloured members of the Partridge series like the Partridge & Yellow. This feather dyes well for the Mayfly patterns.

Of all the feathers used in fly dressing the partridge was by far the most popular: it represented the warm affection that the old country folk had for a bird that was formerly to be found on every farm.

Snipe
An ideal feather for smaller flies requiring grey or dun wings. A feather from the rump of the snipe is a good hackle for the Snipe and Purple.

Starling
An extremely useful bird in that the secondaries and the primaries are used for all the

smaller dun wings. Starling wing fibre is of a good texture to work with. Some body feathers are used for the Black Quill.

Pheasant

The secondaries and primaries of the hen pheasant are used for March Brown and Invicta. Some of the neck feathers of the hen are also used for the Grannom. The neck feathers of the cock are used as hackle for Haul a Gwynt.

Jay

The large primaries, although of a slightly coarse texture, are good dun wings for big flies dressed on a number eight hook. The blue covert feathers are used as hackle for the Haslam and the Invicta.

Teal

The primaries and secondaries are used for dun wings. The barred flank feathers are used extensively on wings of the Teal series of flies. It is also used for the Peter Ross. Some fly dressers use a wigeon flank feather in preference to a teal, because it is often better marked and of better texture. Wigeon feathers do not have the tendency to splay out when tied in.

Peacock

The herls from the long tail are wound around the hook to form a body such as the Coch-a-bon-ddu. The sword feathers are used for wings of the Alexandra and the Marchog Coch.

Body Materials

Fly-dressers who often go to great pains to find the correct hackle for a fly often ignore the importance of the body. Of the two, the body texture and shade is by far the more important

Many of the old traditional patterns used the fur of the hare. The colours obtainable from hare fur are quite extensive. The hare's ear provides the olive fur which is required for many Olive flies. The body fur of a hare gives fur ranging in colour from light ginger to a very dark brown. The Water Rat and the Grey Squirrel also provide good body fur for flies.

Rabbit fur, although similar in texture to that of the hare, is not quite so widely used. The blue fur provides the body of the Grey Duster and the fawn back fur is used for the Sun Fly. The mole's fur, while being of excellent texture to work with, does not have so many patterns that require its limited colour of dark dun. When dyed in Picric acid it gives a very prominent shade of olive.

The best body material for flies is seal's fur. It has the advantage of being shiny and bright even in its wet stage. It dyes well and, although quite hard to work with for beginners, it is well worth taking the trouble to learn how to dub it correctly.

Some fifty years ago dubbing, by and large, was made of wool. The choice was limited in those days and an odd garment seen being worn that took the eye of a fly dresser was in grave danger of disappearing or at least of being shorn. That was the fate of one very attractive scarf in the Ffestiniog area. Even today one pattern bears the name of Egarych sgarff Huw Nain, which was a small Sedge tied with the body made from the scarf of some Huw who was named after his grandmother.

Many novice dressers experience some difficulty with making dubbing bodies. There is a simple way of attaching fur to silk, but, as with all other crafts, there are distinct advantages in doing it the correct way.

Some fly dressers wax the silk before applying the dubbing. If cobbler's wax is used, then the fur will stick to the silk and tend to form rather a lifeless lump of material - like so much putty. Other dressers will just roll the dubbing around the silk and let the fur stand upright and away from the silk. A body formed by such a method allows light to penetrate through the fibres. Experienced dressers only use a small pinch of fur at a time.

When applying the fur to the silk, the fur should be on the first finger and thumb of the working hand. The silk should be held taut from the hook with the other hand. The fur is then placed on the silk - and the thumb and finger should press hard together and twist - twisting the fur and silk together in one direction. Never twist in both directions, as this will unwind the dubbing. Rolling the silk and fur one way will make it onto a long thin cylinder.

Some of the old dressers had another method of making a dubbing body. They would take a pinch of fur and roll it for quite some time between their thumb and first finger, making it into a small ball. They would then tie in this ball with the tying silk. Many would claim that this method, now seldom practised, provided a better body than that made by other methods.

Also available in this series from Merlin Unwin Books

Trout & Salmon

FLIES OF IRELAND

Peter O'Reilly

Hardback, price £20

This is a comprehensive guide to the best contemporary fishing flies for Irish waters. Peter O'Reilly, well-known for his informative books on the rivers and loughs of Ireland, here describes:
• Trout, salmon and seatrout flies for rivers and loughs
• Dry flies, emergers, wet flies, hairwings, mini-tubes etc
• Indigenous Irish patterns, both old and new
• The most successful imported patterns
This book, which includes invaluable tips and advice from local experts, is a must for all anglers in Ireland.

And available from autumn 1997: Trout & Salmon Flies of Scotland

Next day despatch, free UK direct mail service from
Merlin Unwin Books
58 Broad Street
Ludlow, Shropshire SY8 1GQ

Credit card orders: 01584 877456
Fax: 01584 877457